DRIVE: MENTAL TOUGHNESS FOR YOUNG ATHLETES

Mastering the Sports Psychology of Golf

Chase Brooks

Copyright © 2023 by Chase Brooks

All rights reserved.

No portion of this book may be reproduced in any form without written permission from the publisher or author, except as permitted by U.S. copyright law.

contents

Introduction — 1

1. Chapter 1: Mental Toughness in Golf — 5
2. Chapter 2: Skill #1–Staying on Course — 5
3. Chapter 3: Skill #2–Emotional Mastery — 5
4. Chapter 4: Skill #3–Do the Disciplines — 5
5. Chapter 5: Skill #4–Unshakeable Self-Belief — 5
6. Chapter 6: Skill #5—Setting the Right Goals — 5
7. Chapter 7: Skill #6—Patience and Persistence — 5
8. Chapter 8: Skill #7—Bouncing Back from Failure — 5
9. Chapter 9: Skill #8—Practicing Positivity — 5
10. Words of Wisdom to Players — 5
11. Final Note to Coaches — 5
12. References — 5

Introduction

Imagine standing amidst the breathtaking beauty of the Augusta National Golf Club. The vibrant greens glistening under the gentle kiss of the April sun, exuding a mesmerizing radiance. The air is thick with anticipation. The scene is blend of awed silences, bursts of applause, and the soft whispers of commentators narrating a story as old as time: the clash between talent and self-doubt.

Enter Sergio Garcia, the Spanish sensation. For nearly twenty years, Garcia's dance with golf was filled with tantalizingly close calls and dreams just out of reach. The course became his battleground—a place where his prodigious talent often wrestled with a cloud of personal doubts and insecurities. With each swing, the weight of missed opportunities and past failures clung to him. The grandeur of major tournaments seemed to only amplify his inner struggles, painting a tale of almosts and what-ifs.

Sound familiar? Maybe you've felt the same sting of frustration on the green or stared down a scorecard that seemed to mock your dedication. Golf is a rollercoaster—filled with highs of elation and lows of anguish. It's not just about perfecting the swing but taming the tempest within. If you've picked up this book, perhaps you're seeking to unlock the mental mastery of golf, turning obstacles into launch pads and aiming not just for success, but for unparalleled greatness.

As you journey through the pages of this book, you'll be embarking on a voyage of self-discovery, diving into the crevices of your psyche, and coming up with pearls of wisdom. It's not merely about mastering the physicality of golf—learning how to swing a club with precision or understanding the fine mechanics of a perfect putt. This journey is about a metamorphosis of the mind—it's about embracing resilience, cultivating patience, and reprogramming your reactions to setbacks. You'll be introduced to eight critical skills, each designed to unlock a different aspect of your mental game, transforming you into a better golfer, a better competitor, and a more focused individual.

These lessons are the result of years spent studying and observing the world's most successful golfers to understand the mental fortitude that underscores their sterling performances. We've dissected the mindsets of athletes like Tiger Woods, Phil Mickelson, and Gaby Lopez, who, despite being under the unforgiving lens of public scrutiny, have navigated the turbulent seas of their careers with unyielding mental toughness. The stories, skills, and strategies that you'll discover are not just abstract theories confined within the covers of this book. They are practical, actionable steps that have been implemented by these golfing greats, carving paths to their remarkable achievements.

Take Tiger Woods, for instance—a golfer who doesn't just play the sport; he transcends it. Tiger's name is synonymous with golf, his prowess echoing through every fairway around the world. But his journey wasn't just about perfecting a swing or mastering a putt. Tiger's tale is one of sheer grit and unyielding mental strength. From public scandals to crippling injuries, Tiger's career has been a roller coaster, replete with dizzying highs and despairing lows. Yet, he returned, time and again, his resilience turning adversities into championships, proving that mental toughness was as essential to his arsenal as his clubs.

Or consider the narrative of Phil Mickelson, another legend of the links. Mickelson's career is a testament to the power of a positive mindset. Faced with a six-year major drought and the moniker of "best player to never win a major," Phil refused to succumb to the rising tide of negativity. Instead, he channeled it, molding it into a force that propelled him toward greatness, culminating in his triumph at the 2004 Masters. Phil's journey serves as a compelling argument for the effectiveness of the strategies we will explore in the following chapters.

Similarly, Gaby Lopez's story further corroborates the importance of mental toughness. Lopez, an LPGA professional, often points out that her most significant victories occur off the golf course, in the gym, where she trains her mind to endure, to focus, and to overcome. Her rigorous mental conditioning, just as much as her physical training, has been instrumental in shaping her into the golfer she is today.

Recalling our first example, in 2017, Garcia emerged from the shadows, not just as a maestro with his clubs, but as a warrior of the mind. Triumphing at the Masters, he showcased a newfound mental resilience—a transformation from a golfer who once wavered under pressure to one radiating serene confidence. This wasn't mere luck but the result of mastering the oft-ignored aspect of golf: Mental Toughness.

Each chapter of this book is designed to guide you toward mirroring these feats of mental fortitude in your game. You'll delve into harnessing the power of focus, understanding the role of failure, learning to cope with pressure, and developing the ability to adapt—all essential elements that transform a good golfer into a great one. By the time you turn the final page, you'll have a comprehensive understanding of the mental game of golf. More importantly, you'll have a roadmap that you can follow, complete with actionable strategies, relatable anecdotes, and evidence-based techniques. This is not just a book; it is a transformative journey that will lead you to a better version of yourself both on and off the course.

So, why this book, you might ask? It's a valid question. The market teems with resources, each promising the secret formula to mastering golf. What sets this book apart isn't the promise of a miracle cure. Instead, it's the assurance of a methodical, holistic approach to understanding the mental aspect of golf—an approach gleaned from extensive research, interviews, and an immersive study of the most successful minds in golf.

This book is your key to decoding the mental mysteries of golf. With each turn of the page, you'll embark on a transformative journey. You'll understand the interplay of psychological and physical elements in golf, how the resilience of your mind can shape the precision of your swing, and how a positive mindset can transform the trajectory of your shot.

This is your invitation to embark on a journey that transcends the physical boundaries of golf and dives into the intricate labyrinth of the mental game. Prepare to unveil a side of golf that has remained in the shadows for too long. Let's journey together from the confounding depths of despair to the exhilarating heights of success, navigating the intricate terrain of the mental game of golf. This is not just about becoming a better golfer. It's about becoming a better you.

Chapter 1: Mental Toughness in Golf

As the sun dips below the horizon, painting the sky with hues of burnt orange and crimson, the hushed whisper of the wind rustling the leaves accompanies the last hole of a grueling golf match. The ball teeters on the edge of the 18th hole, a mere stroke away from victory or defeat. The golfer, standing amid the silent audience and the watchful cameras, readies himself for the final shot. Sweating palms, elevated heart rate, and a cacophony of thoughts—yet it is here, in this crucible of pressure, that the golfer must summon his calm, marshal his focus, and make his play. The lesson of this story? Jack Nicklaus was onto something when he declared, "Don't ever try to tell me golf is not 99.9 percent a mental game."

Few understand the intense mental warfare waged on the greens better than Jack Nicklaus, recognized by many as an exceptional golfer of unprecedented stature. His impressive career was not merely a testament to physical skill or technical proficiency. It was his relentless belief in his abilities, his laser-sharp focus on what he could control, and his unwavering determination to continually improve himself that led him to victory after victory. As we explore the labyrinthine depths of mental toughness in golf, we'll uncover the essence of what Nicklaus meant: that golf, more than most sports, is a battle fought primarily within the golfer's mind.

So, what does it mean to be mentally tough in golf? It's a mosaic composed of acceptance, patience, self-confidence, composure, focus, and control, each piece having its own role to play in the broader picture. Imagine your mind as a garden, where each character is a seed that must be carefully nurtured and cultivated to grow into its full potential. We will walk through this garden, examining each element and showing how they are applied in the challenging world of golf.

One might wonder why golf is considered more mentally demanding than other sports. To put it simply, golf gives you an abundance of time to think but demands that every shot count. How does a golfer find balance amidst these constraints, juggling consistency with the inevitable frustrations that arise? What are the misconceptions around "emotional control?" Can positivity be used correctly to boost performance? All these questions, and more, will be answered as we delve into the mental mechanics of the game.

However, despite the complex interplay of emotions, thoughts, and actions, there is no "secret" formula to mastering the mental game. Just like a physical skill, mental toughness requires rigorous and consistent practice. It's about showing up each day, willing to learn, ready to grow, and committed to refining your mental approach. One bad day on the golf course doesn't define your game, but how you recover and learn from it does.

This might sound daunting, but mental toughness also brings a plethora of benefits. It grants you a key to the elusive "zone," allowing you to remain composed under pressure, to refocus after a bad shot, and ultimately to enhance your enjoyment of the game. Timing, which plays a crucial role, cannot be overlooked when applying these mental skills. It is essential to master the art of being patient yet alert and calm yet focused, as well as to maintain an unwavering vision of the bigger picture, no matter the challenges of the present moment.

Throughout this book, we invite you to embark on a journey, one that transcends the physical boundaries of golf to explore the realm of the intangible. Let's look at the story of Collin Morikawa, a rising star in the golf world, and his coach, Rick Sessinghaus. Their unique relationship offers a compelling study of how mental toughness can be nurtured and utilized in golf, a testament to the irreplaceable role the mind plays in the pursuit of greatness.

In the end, whether you're a teenager aiming to become a professional golfer or a parent encouraging your child's passion, this journey will provide valuable insights into the psychological battleground that defines the game of golf. So, come along. Let's tee off into the mysterious, challenging, and rewarding world of mental toughness in golf.

It's a Game of Mind

In the mind of golfing legend Jack Nicklaus, mental toughness is not just an asset, it's the secret sauce that separates the good from the great. Beyond powerful swings and perfect putts, Nicklaus insists that the game of golf is fundamentally a test of mental resilience. This comes as no surprise, as his own legendary career bore testament to this principle time and again. As you take on the challenge of golf or any aspect of life, consider Nicklaus' personal principles and beliefs about mental toughness.

From his first encounter with a golf club to his record-setting victories, Nicklaus emphasized one thing above all: the power of self-belief. For him, mental strength was not about ignoring distractions, but rather about focusing on the self. He expressed the view that physical strength might be a valuable asset, but it's the unshaken belief in oneself that can truly set a player apart. This ability to tune out external noise and zoom in on personal capability can help not only in maintaining focus but also in minimizing distractions on the golf course.

Nicklaus once said, "I think you've got to believe in what you can do," shedding light on the importance of not comparing oneself to others. It's not about what someone else can do; it's about what *you* can do. This viewpoint underscores the significance of personal growth and self-improvement. Nicklaus's emphasis on working within oneself and improving one's own skills and abilities is a testament to his approach to greatness. It's not a single victory that defines you but how you grow and improve over the long haul.

Speaking of mental toughness, it's worth noting that it's not something you're born with but rather something that you develop and strengthen over time. Nicklaus' career is a case study of this development. Known for his incredible longevity and consistency in the sport, he won his first major at 22 and his last at 46, demonstrating the power of a strong mental game over a long, challenging career. Remember, teens and parents alike, mental toughness and a strong belief in oneself are skills that extend far beyond the golf course. They are applicable in every aspect of life, from dealing with academic pressure to navigating social situations and even future career paths. Nicklaus' wisdom, gathered from a storied career, serves as valuable advice: Believe in your abilities, focus on self-improvement, and always, always play the long game.

Just as Jack Nicklaus harnessed the power of his mind to rise to the peak of golf, each of us has the potential to use our mental strength to achieve our personal best. It's about discipline, resilience, and an unwavering belief in oneself. So, when you step onto the golf course or face a challenge in life, remember to channel your inner Jack Nicklaus and play your own game.

What Mental Toughness Means in Golf

Mental toughness, particularly in the context of golf, encapsulates a variety of psychological strengths that significantly influence performance. These strengths range from self-confidence to patience, and their importance cannot be overstated. This chapter explores the characteristics of mental toughness in golf and offers practical examples of their application.

Self-Confidence

In golf, self-confidence plays a pivotal role in fueling performance. Every golfer's journey is marked by highs and lows; a hole-in-one today could be followed by a series of missed shots tomorrow. For instance, consider the professional golfer Phil Mickelson who started the final day of a British Open competition five shots off the lead. Yet, his unwavering self-confidence, undeterred by the odds, propelled him to victory. Such resilience in the face of adversity is essential in building a golfer's mental toughness. Confidence in one's abilities, despite previous missteps, can often determine the success of the next swing.

Composure

Golf can be a roller-coaster ride of emotions, with exhilarating highs and frustrating lows. When faced with a tough round or an unfortunate shot, the ability to maintain composure is invaluable. For example, imagine the tension of a professional golfer, live on national television, faced with a crucial putt to win the championship. A mentally tough golfer will not allow frustration or disappointment to disrupt their game but will rather use these emotions as motivation to continue and improve.

Focus

Golf is often a marathon rather than a sprint, requiring a golfer to remain focused for hours on end. Golf courses are riddled with distractions, from weather conditions to the noise of spectators. Mental toughness demands an ability to focus exclusively on the task at hand, dismissing both external and internal distractions. Let's take an example of a golfer standing on the 18th tee, tied for the lead, with a roaring crowd in the background. A mentally tough golfer will successfully block out these distractions, instead focusing on their swing, the ball's trajectory, and their strategy for this vital shot.

Control

Control is the culmination of self-confidence, composure, and focus. It means being the master of your thoughts and actions on the course and not letting frustration or doubt hinder your performance. Imagine a scenario where a golfer is faced with a challenging shot over a water hazard. In this instance, a golfer exhibiting mental toughness will remain in control, focusing their attention on the shot at hand rather than on the potential for a penalty.

Patience

The game of golf also requires a great deal of patience. Sometimes, a golfer may not perform as well as they'd like, or progress may be slower than expected. Patience is evident when a golfer, despite having a rough first few holes, maintains their cool and sticks to their strategy, understanding that golf is a game of highs and lows and that things can turn around in their favor at any moment.

Acceptance

Golf, like life, does not always go as planned. Even professional golfers miss shots and experience rounds that seem to go awry from the first swing. Acceptance in golf is about acknowledging these moments, learning from them, and moving on without self-criticism. An example of this might be a golfer who, after missing what seemed like an easy putt, does not dwell on their mistake. Instead, they accept it, learn from it, and move on to the next hole with renewed determination.

In conclusion, mental toughness in golf is a blend of various psychological attributes that work in unison to enhance performance. Just like physical training, these mental skills can be developed and honed over time. As a young golfer, cultivating these characteristics can pave the way not only for a successful golfing career but also for a healthier and more balanced life. For parents supporting these young athletes, understanding these attributes can help encourage a mindset of resilience, patience, and self-belief, valuable traits that extend beyond the golf course.

It's Tougher Than Other Sports

In the world of sports, there exists one sport, nestled among other competitive activities, that holds a different kind of challenge. This game dares to test the mental agility of its players more than any other. This sport is golf.

What makes golf unique is the manner in which it interlaces the physical with the mental, creating a fusion that demands more than just athleticism. This is why even the most physically gifted athletes from other sports struggle when trying to play golf professionally. Figures like Tony Romo, Michael Jordan, Ivan Lendl, and John Smoltz, all exceptional athletes in their own rights, found it difficult to compete in golf at the highest level, despite their established athletic prowess.

To explain the challenge that golf poses, we need to understand the key attributes that separate it from other sports:

1. Lots of Time to Think: In most sports, players need to make split-second decisions. There's an urgency that requires quick reactions. In golf, however, the ball isn't moving. You have a lot of time to think, to consider each shot, and to prepare to swing. This ability to ponder over each move often leads to overthinking, and overthinking, as we know, can disrupt the natural flow of play.

2. Every Shot Counts: In other sports, perfection isn't expected. A baseball player is considered successful even if he only hits a third of the pitches thrown at him. In golf, however, every shot matters. The outcome of each stroke significantly impacts the overall score, adding an extra layer of pressure that can easily interfere with a player's mental state.

3. Balancing Consistency with Frustration: Golf requires consistency, but it also inspires a fair amount of frustration. Players are encouraged to follow a consistent routine before each shot, focusing on the minutiae of steps, waggles, alignment checks, and more. This pursuit of consistency, though, often leads to frustration, particularly when, despite all efforts, the shots don't go as planned.

4. Levels of Arousal: The level of arousal (which refers to a person's state of physical alertness and mental readiness) changes the dynamics of a golf swing. If the level of arousal on the course is different from that during practice, the swing may

not feel right or work as effectively. This fluctuation can add to the mental challenge of the game.

Beyond these factors, golf also requires dealing with an immense array of variables: from learning to use 14 different clubs in more than 14 ways to adjusting to various types of grass, green speeds, weather conditions, and more. Then there's the matter of playing over a period of four to six hours, over several rounds, with conditions that can change dramatically.

Also, don't forget that golf is an individual sport. There are no teammates to rely on, no one to pass the responsibility to. The burden of every decision, every stroke, falls squarely on the shoulders of the individual player. This lack of support can amplify the mental strain, making golf a mentally tougher sport compared to most others.

All of this emphasizes the need to approach golf not just as a physical sport but also as a mental challenge. It's a game that asks its players to navigate a maze of thoughts, emotions, pressures, and decisions, all while trying to perfect a skill that is often counterintuitive and extremely demanding. Understanding and mastering the mental aspect of golf thus becomes a key part of any player's journey toward success. And as with all journeys, it is one best navigated one stroke at a time.

Common Myths About Mental Toughness

Mental toughness is an essential component of success, not just in sports but in many aspects of life. However, there are common myths and misconceptions about mental toughness, emotional control, the use of positivity, and the idea of consistency that can confuse and hinder our understanding and development of these skills. Let's dive into each of these topics, tailor-made for a teenage audience and their parents.

Breaking Down Misconceptions

Many people believe that working on one's mental game, or mental toughness, is an admission of weakness or deficiency. However, this is far from the truth. Mental toughness is not about exposing and repairing faults but about building skills, much like practicing to improve at a sport or an instrument. The essence lies in acquiring the ability to maintain concentration on the current undertaking, to remain mindful and fully engaged. This skill is not about addressing a "weakness;" rather, it's about enhancing your strengths and abilities to handle pressure and stress effectively.

The Stigma Around the Mental Game

One common myth is the belief that our minds can be completely controlled and that we can create a mental bubble where only positive thoughts exist. However, even the most successful athletes and individuals can't control every thought that pops into their heads. Instead, they've learned to control their reactions to their thoughts. It's crucial to understand that having a random negative thought doesn't mean you're failing at the mental game. What matters is how you handle these thoughts—acknowledging them, letting them pass, and refocusing on the task at hand.

The Misconception Around "Emotional Control"

Many people think that emotional control means suppressing or denying feelings, especially negative ones. However, emotional control doesn't mean not having emotions. It's about recognizing and understanding your emotions and then managing how you react to them. For example, experiencing pre-game jitters doesn't indicate weakness; rather, it is a natural reaction to a high-pressure scenario. Emotional control comes in when you use strategies to prevent those nerves from negatively affecting your performance.

Using Positivity Correctly

Many believe that merely thinking positively will lead to positive results. However, simply repeating "I'm going to ace this test" or "I'm going to win this match" doesn't guarantee success. It's more helpful to use positive questioning, such as "What does a successful outcome look like?" or "What steps can I take to perform at my best?" These types of questions focus on the process and help create a constructive mindset without promising a specific outcome.

The Myth of Consistency

Many people believe that maintaining a consistent state of mind will lead to consistent performance. However, life is full of variables (such as our physical condition, mood, and environment), and all these factors can change daily, affecting our performance. Instead of chasing a mythical consistency, it's more beneficial to cultivate adaptability, the ability to adjust and perform well under varying circumstances.

The "Secret" to Winning in the Mind

The realm of the mind has always been a fascinating one, especially in sports psychology. The concept of mental toughness stands as an elusive yet powerful factor contributing to the success or failure of athletes. There's a common misconception that there exists a "secret" formula to mastering this toughness; however, the reality isn't shrouded in mystery.

Mental toughness isn't a secret ingredient that one suddenly stumbles upon. Rather, it's a progressive evolution of mindset and character. Like a muscle, it needs constant and consistent training to become strong and resilient. It's the repeated habits and mindset shifts, reinforced over time, that build mental toughness.

Consider the story of Phil Mickelson, a revered figure in golf. Phil endured numerous setbacks and was often so close to the brink of victory, only to have it slip away. It took him 12 years to win his first major, but he persevered. He kept grinding, improving his game piece by piece, eventually winning multiple major titles. His journey wasn't marked by an elusive secret but by sheer perseverance, patience, and a strong mindset. You can train your mind to be tough too. Here are some practical steps to follow:

1. Winning in the Mind: The journey to victory is as much about developing mental fortitude as it is about honing physical skills. Look at Phil Mickelson's trajectory. It took him time, resilience, and mental toughness to finally win a major title after years of setbacks.

2. No "Secret" to Mental Toughness: Building mental toughness isn't about a secret formula. It's about consistent practice and persistence. Just like you have to physically train to become a better golfer, you must also train your mind to become mentally stronger.

3. The Past Doesn't Define You: It doesn't matter what happened yesterday, whether you made a mistake, had a setback, or achieved a victory. The key to mental toughness is focusing on the present and bringing your best self to the current game.

4. No Single Skill is the Magic Pill: Mental toughness isn't about mastering one skill but about mastering a combination of them. It's about using these skills in unison with your mindset rather than allowing them to conflict.

5. Master Your Breathing: A critical part of mental toughness is controlling your breathing, especially during stressful moments. This helps reset your mind and body, allowing you to maintain a clear focus and a calm demeanor.

6. Maintain Positive Body Language: Maintaining an upbeat physical demeanor, irrespective of your performance, assists in keeping a serene mindset. This mental toughness trait helps you to not dwell on the past and to focus on the next move.

7. Monitor Your Self-Talk: Be mindful of what you're saying to yourself on the course. Replace negative self-talk with neutral or positive statements that keep your morale high and your focus sharp.

8. Use Neutral Thinking: Moving from negative to neutral thinking, as suggested by mental coach Trevor Moawad, can help you avoid dwelling on bad shots and keep your mind focused.

9. Celebrate Positive Shots: Remember and relish your successful shots. By keeping these positive memories at the forefront, you can push past challenges more easily.

10. Laugh Off Bad Shots: Don't get overly emotional about bad shots. It's better to brush them off and focus on the next one, helping you keep a cool head and a steady pace.

11. Keep a Mental Game Scorecard: Rather than solely focusing on the result, obsess over the process. You can create a mental game scorecard that gives you points based on your mental

preparation and execution rather than on the result of the shot.

12. Stop Worrying About the Score: Sometimes, it's beneficial to set aside the scorecard and focus on enjoying the game. This can relieve pressure and allow you to perform more naturally.

13. Stop Comparing Yourself to Others: Comparing yourself to others often leads to discontent and pressure. Focus on your own progress and growth instead.

14. Post-Round Recap: After each round, take a few minutes to reflect on the game. Note down both your best shots and the areas you need to improve. This helps keep your focus on continuous improvement.

15. Read Golf Books: Reading can provide you with a new perspective, help you break away from old thought patterns, and upgrade your mindset.

16. Take a Break if Needed: If you're feeling overwhelmed, taking a break can be beneficial. It can help you reset, regain your focus, and reignite your love for the game.

In summary, the "secret" to winning in mind and building mental toughness isn't a secret at all. It's a journey of consistent practice, mindset shifts, and skill development. Remember, it's not about what happened yesterday; it's about how you show up today. It's about what you do over and over again that shapes your mental toughness. There's no quick fix–it's a continuous journey of growth, improvement, and resilience.

Power Your Swing With Mental Toughness

Have you ever wondered why some players manage to deliver remarkable performances consistently, while others, despite possessing excellent skills and talent, fail to reach their potential? The answer lies not in their physical prowess but in their mental toughness. The essence of golf, especially at higher levels, is in the power of the mind.

In golf, each swing is set up by decisions, thoughts, images, and feelings. Mental training complements the mechanics or physical aspects of the game, aiding players in maintaining confidence, trust, focus, and composure—the cornerstone of mental toughness. Although it's a common misconception, mental conditioning isn't solely for athletes battling difficulties with their performance but is also beneficial for those seeking to enhance their overall game proficiency.

The Zoning Advantage

When golfers exhibit exceptional control, composure, confidence, and focus on the course, we say they are "in the zone." Most golfers have experienced the zone, albeit temporarily. Nevertheless, the ability to cultivate a mental state that permits more regular entry into the zone is a skill that's accessible to everyone. The key is to understand how to maintain focus, confidence, and control.

Mentally tough golfers enjoy numerous advantages during the competition:

1. Awareness of the Zone: They identify the sensations linked with being in the zone and have the capability to immerse themselves in it deliberately.

2. High Self-Confidence: They hold firm confidence in their capabilities and their potential to deliver excellent performance.

3. Concentration: They can immerse themselves fully in the task at hand, concentrating solely on the present.

4. Focused Attention: They can narrow their attention to focus on one specific thought without distraction.

5. Effortless Execution: They can swing effortlessly and let things happen when it counts.

6. Emotional Control: They remain calm under pressure and demonstrate emotional stability.

7. Clear Decision-Making: They avoid overthinking, doubt, and indecision.

8. Refocusing Ability: They can quickly refocus and collect themselves after a mistake or a bad shot.

9. Fun: Regardless of their score, they find enjoyment in playing the game.

Commitment to Developing Mental Toughness

Developing mental toughness isn't a one-time activity—it requires a daily commitment over weeks, months, and even years. The essential aspect is to consistently incorporate a mental strategy into both training sessions and competitive events. That's why top golf coaches now stress the importance of mental training.

In golf, cultivating mental fortitude extends beyond a mere mindset and becomes an integral part of one's lifestyle. The discipline, confidence, and focus it fosters enable golfers to be fully immersed in the present, effortlessly execute their swing, and calmly handle mounting pressure. The mentally tough golfer makes clear, decisive decisions and recovers swiftly from setbacks. Remember, every stroke you make in golf involves decisions: considering the distance, selecting the appropriate club, analyzing the wind direction, deciding how far to aim to the right or left, and anticipating the roll of the ball on the ground. Having mental toughness equips you to make these decisions confidently and accurately.

Just as you practice your swing and strategize your game, developing mental toughness should be a vital part of your training regime. It's not about achieving a perfect swing; it's about building a strong, resilient mindset that will empower you to improve your game and enjoy it even more.

Remember the words of Bob Rotella, sport psychologist: "Believe you can win, stay in the present, remain patient, and ignore advice from well-meaning friends." If you've done the work to develop your mental toughness, be confident in your abilities and stick to your game plan. After all, mental toughness is the secret sauce that can make the difference between a good golfer and a great one.

Timing is Everything

Every aspect of golf revolves around timing. The correct sequencing of body movements in your swing, the rhythm of your putts, and even the moment you choose to take your shot all require impeccable timing. However, the concept extends further than just the physical execution. Strategic timing is equally important in golf. Knowing when to play it safe and when to take risks, when to attack the pin, and when to aim for the middle of the green–these decisions can make a significant difference in your game. It's about understanding the state of the game and making choices that optimize your chances of success.

Understanding timing also relates to your mental state. Golf requires patience and the ability to remain focused under pressure. If you rush your decisions or let your frustration control your actions, your game can quickly unravel. Learning to manage your emotions and maintain a steady pace, regardless of the situation, is a key aspect of mastering timing in golf.

The Importance of Mental Toughness

Recognizing the right moments to practice mental toughness can dramatically affect your game. It's during high-pressure situations where mental toughness truly shines, whether that's on the golf course or during a challenging day at school or work. Embrace every challenge as an opportunity to grow mentally tougher. Whether it's a hard shot, a challenging hole, or a difficult day, each situation is a chance to flex your mental muscles.

The Art of Long-Term Thinking

While being mentally tough at the right moment is crucial, so is sticking to your bigger game plan. It's essential not to lose sight of the long-term goal while managing the short-term hurdles. The strategy is to play the long game—to keep your eyes on the end goal while navigating the immediate challenges.

Leave the Past Behind

Dwelling on the past—a poor shot or a missed opportunity—can derail your current game. Each shot should be approached independently of the previous ones, with fresh eyes and a renewed focus. Learn from your mistakes, yes, but don't let them color your current play.

Breathing and Building Routines

Breathing can be a powerful tool in maintaining composure and alleviating tension. Before every shot, take a moment to breathe deeply and steady your nerves. This simple routine can help clear your mind and keep you grounded in the present.

Consistency breeds excellence. Building routines for each phase of your game turns them into habits, making them second nature. This way, even under immense pressure, you'll fall back on a well-practiced routine that you can trust.

Deliberate Practice

It's not mere practice that leads to perfection, but the perfection of practice itself. The emphasis should be on the caliber of the practice session rather than on its duration. Slow down your practice sessions to focus on each aspect of your game, from visualizing the swing to hitting the ball. This is the embodiment of the principle "go slow to go fast."

Trusting Your Process

Having a shot routine and a process that you trust is invaluable. Whether it's a simple routine or a complex one, the key is to trust in your method and use it with every single shot—especially after the not-so-good ones. It's about unwavering commitment, just like the pros have.

Mental Skills Development

It's not a lack of technical expertise that often holds golfers back, but a lack of mental toughness. Recognizing this and working on developing key mental skills from a young age is a cornerstone to a successful golf career and a resilient approach to life.

These are the foundational aspects of mental toughness in golf and in life. Mastering them isn't just about improving your game; it's about enhancing your overall mental fortitude. Remember, you're not just a golfer on the course; you're a warrior in the game of life.

These lessons are not just about becoming a better golfer but about becoming a more resilient and confident individual. They teach you how to navigate the game of life, understand your strengths, and manage your weaknesses. The principles of timing, mental toughness, long-term thinking, focusing on the present, embracing the uncontrollable, and playing to succeed can guide you not just on the green but in every aspect of life.

Stories to Inspire: The "Intangible" Part of Golf

In a realm where physical prowess often overshadows the hidden factors that make a champion, one tale stands out. This is the story of Collin Morikawa, a prodigy of the greens, and his lifelong mentor Rick Sessinghaus, who believed that mastering the mind was equally as vital as mastering the swing. Collin Morikawa first joined forces with Sessinghaus when Collin was just eight years old. With a natural flair for golf, Morikawa presented great promise, but Sessinghaus, an applied sports psychologist, believed that there was an "intangible" that could elevate Morikawa's game to the next level. This intangible was no physical skill or perfected technique but rather the "mental game," an often-overlooked aspect of competitive sports.

With a unique perspective on the game, Sessinghaus nurtured young Collin, focusing more on the psychological side than on the physical. Morikawa remembers vividly one lesson from his mentor: the power of word choice. "Rick has taught me so much mentally," Morikawa says, "but I think the one thing that really sticks with me is how important word choice is. If we talk about the word 'nerves,' everyone has them, but how can you mentally change that nervousness into excitement or focus?" The impact of this mindset became exceptionally evident during the 70th hole of the PGA Championship, as Morikawa exceeded all expectations with a remarkable stroke that left an indelible mark in the annals of major championship history. Faced with a moment that could have been debilitatingly tense, Morikawa instead transformed his nerves into focus, propelling him to victory and offering sweet validation for Sessinghaus's teachings.

A considerable part of Morikawa's education with Sessinghaus was spent not on the driving range but on the course itself. Sessinghaus believes in the value of applied learning, making Morikawa practice under varied conditions, challenging him constantly, and bringing out his creative side. "Being creative and hitting different shots with different lies taught me to think about the options available instead of just making the same full swing every time, like on the range," Morikawa explains.

Sessinghaus also introduced Morikawa to the concept of "flow state," a state of total absorption where performance peaks and the mind functions on autopilot. While many deem this state as elusive and transient, Sessinghaus imparted to Morikawa that it is possible to train for this state, to understand its triggers, and to replicate it.

The culmination of Sessinghaus' teachings came into play during the final round of the PGA. Sessinghaus, alongside Morikawa's agent, had a front-row seat to watch their pupil masterfully navigate the course. "It was quite a journey," he says, referring not just to that triumphant day but also to the 15 years of laborious work they had put in together.

In a world where success is often defined by physical feats, the journey of Collin Morikawa and Rick Sessinghaus serves as a compelling reminder that there is much more to winning than meets the eye. The intangible, the mental game, can often be the difference between a good player and a champion, a lesson every young athlete and their parents can take to heart.

Teeing Up: Actionable Steps to Improve Mental Toughness

Now that we've covered the importance and role of mental toughness in golf, it's time to provide you with some actionable steps to help enhance your mental strength on the course. We're going to split these strategies into two categories: for the coach and for the athlete. Implementing these techniques can provide a practical framework for applying the lessons learned in this chapter.

For the Coach

1. Build a growth mindset: Stress the importance of a growth mindset to your athletes. Teach them that every round, every hole, and every shot is an opportunity to learn and grow. Emphasize that failure is not a setback but a chance to improve.

2. Establish consistent routines: Encourage your athletes to build routines for each phase of the game, from pre-shot to post-shot. Routines help build mental toughness, as they allow the athlete to focus on the process rather than on the outcome.

3. Encourage mental practice: Promote the idea of mental practice. This could include visualization exercises, meditation, and mental rehearsal of tough situations. This will help athletes become mentally prepared and resilient.

4. Challenge beliefs: Open dialogues around commonly held myths and misconceptions about mental toughness in golf. Debunk these myths and promote healthy, constructive beliefs about mental toughness.

5. Foster resilience: Foster a resilience mindset in your athletes by reminding them to take each shot one at a time and to

not dwell on past performances. Encourage them to see challenges as opportunities for growth.

For the Athlete

1. Adopt a mindset of growth: Recognize that you possess the inherent ability to continuously enhance yourself, and view every failure as a valuable stepping stone on the path to achievement.

2. Establish and maintain routines: Routines provide stability and consistency, helping you focus and remain calm under pressure. Develop routines that work for you and stick to them.

3. Practice mental skills: Regularly perform mental exercises like visualization and mindfulness meditation. These can help build mental toughness by training your brain to stay focused and composed.

4. Challenge your beliefs: Confront any misconceptions or unhealthy beliefs you may have about mental toughness. Replace these with constructive, empowering beliefs.

5. Cultivate resilience: Remember that resilience is key in golf. Learn to bounce back from difficult shots and rounds by viewing them as opportunities to learn and grow, not as failures.

Remember, mental toughness is not a destination but a journey. It's about what you do consistently, over and over again. It's about showing up, doing the work, and continually striving to improve, both mentally and physically. Keep practicing, stay focused, and let your mental strength lead you to success on the golf course.

Conclusion

Chapter 1 underscores the critical role that mental toughness plays in golf and in life. It details core principles of mental toughness, including maintaining focus during high-pressure situations, thinking long-term while navigating immediate challenges, leaving past mistakes behind, and engaging in deliberate practice. The importance of building routines and trusting one's process is also emphasized. These elements are vividly portrayed through the compelling story of golfer Collin Morikawa and his mentor Rick Sessinghaus, exemplifying the transformative power of a strong mental game. Finally, the first mental toughness skill, focus, emerges as an essential component in cultivating resilience and success both in golf and in life.

Chapter 2: Skill #1-Staying on Course

"There's a power in letting the world around you become a blur, finding that focal point in the distance, and aligning all your thoughts, your movements, your every breath to reach it. A golfer's mantra could be summed up in Patrick Reed's words: 'I'm not out there to play Rory [McIlroy]. I'm out there to play the golf course.'"

Patrick Reed, a towering figure in the world of golf, isn't battling another player; he's battling the course, the distractions, the pressure, and his own mind. To him, golf is an intricate dance of precision, patience, and mental toughness. This chapter will give you a closer look at Reed's principles and beliefs around maintaining focus in golf and the key role that mental toughness plays in it. By borrowing from his playbook, you can equip yourself to stay on course, both on the golf green and in the game of life. A large part of Reed's strategy is understanding what to focus on, what to tune out, and how not to force your mind into a certain place. One of the guiding principles of his approach is focusing on the process, not the outcome. This is akin to treating golf like a marathon, not a sprint. It's not just about a single shot, a single hole, or a single round; it's about the cumulative result of all the shots, all the holes, all the rounds.

But how do you know what to focus on in this great marathon of golf? And even more importantly, how do you maintain that focus? Let's break it down.

In golf, visualizing the trajectory of the ball and knowing exactly where you want it to go is essential. It's not just about physical precision; it's about mental precision, too. It's about honing your focus on what's in your control and going inward to narrow your attention to specific windows of time. This can lead to better shots and improved performance. Staying focused is a skill that needs to be developed and maintained. And it's not just about what happens on the course; what happens off it plays a crucial role, too. Balancing between quiet spots for mental breaks and practicing on busier courses can help build resilience against distractions.

To further enhance your focus in golf, it's helpful to understand the three types of attention or focus: internal, external, and neutral. Each has a unique effect on your game, and understanding how to leverage each can give you an edge on the golf course. Finally, let's take inspiration from Tiger Woods, a legendary golfer renowned for his mental fortitude and focus. Woods was known for practicing with distractions rather than in silence, a unique approach that helped him maintain his cool in the most challenging of tournaments.

The game of golf, just like life, requires focus, patience, and an ability to tune out distractions. This chapter will provide you with the tools to keep your eye on the ball, stay on course, and navigate through life's challenges, one stroke at a time.

A Formula for Focus

"Focus on the process, not the outcome." This statement, easy to say but difficult to implement, is at the heart of the winning approach adopted by Patrick Reed, a world-class golfer. Reed has demonstrated time and time again that it is mental toughness and a relentless focus on the present that sets him apart. His journey through the Master's Tournament, amid formidable competition and intense pressure, was a testament to this. When asked about the competition, Reed retorted, "I'm out there to play the golf course." That's the philosophy we will be focusing on in this chapter.

Focus on The Process, Not the Outcome

Reed's approach to focus is something to take a lesson from. In the heat of the game, his focus was never on his competitors or on the leaderboard; it was on the game itself. Reed didn't waste his mental energy on things he couldn't control; instead, he focused on what he *could* control: his swings, his strategy, and his responses to challenges. This is the crux of a formula for focus: understanding what to focus on and what to ignore and tuning into what truly matters.

As much as we would like, we can't always force our minds into a specific place or mindset. It's normal for your mind to wander and dwell on potential outcomes, mistakes, or the competition. But as Reed demonstrated, the trick is to recognize when this happens and gently steer your focus back to the task at hand. This process isn't about forcibly quieting your mind but rather about observing your thoughts and then consciously redirecting your focus to the present.

Tuning into what matters is about feeling what's going on around you and within you but not getting caught up in it. Reed was aware of the competition and the pressure that came with it, but he didn't let it deter him from his game. Instead, he used it to fuel his focus and reinforce his commitment to his performance.

Focusing on the Long-term Perspective

This brings us to an important point: focusing on the long-term perspective. Reed's approach was not merely about focusing on the moment but also about focusing on his broader journey. He viewed each tournament as a marathon, not a sprint, reminding us that it's not about instant success or failure but about the bigger picture. A single missed shot doesn't define a game, and a single game doesn't define a career. Finally, focusing on the process, not the outcome, is paramount. This means immersing yourself in what you're doing without obsessing over what you're hoping to achieve. Reed demonstrated this during the 2018 Masters Tournament, focusing on his game instead of worrying about winning. Similarly, golfer Mo Martin displayed incredible focus at the 2014 British Open, focusing on each shot instead of on the tournament outcome.

To emulate this focus, be aware of when your mind starts to drift toward outcomes. Recognize the signs, such as increased anxiety or wandering thoughts, and consciously bring your focus back to the present. Consider each shot, each decision, and each moment as a step in the process, not as a definitive factor in the outcome. Remember that focusing on the process is about doing your best in the present, not about predicting or controlling the future. It's about giving your all to each shot, each moment, trusting in your skills and your training, and accepting whatever outcome comes with grace and resilience. As Reed and Martin have shown us, this approach can lead to surprising and gratifying success.

Knowing What to Focus On

The pursuit of excellence in golf, as with many areas of life, is a lesson in focus. A wandering mind is seldom a successful one when the goal is to master the game of golf. This is a sport that requires a remarkable degree of concentration and awareness. Whether it's identifying the right club to use, analyzing the terrain, or dealing with the nerves of a crucial shot, your mental state can profoundly impact your performance.

Understanding what to focus on and what to tune out in golf is essential. As our expert Kathy Nyman rightly points out, you can't always choose your environment, especially your playing partners. The goal is to foster an internal locus of control, where external distractions like people's behavior or weather conditions have minimal impact on your gameplay. This doesn't mean ignoring these factors entirely; rather, it's about acknowledging them without letting them disrupt your focus.

Focusing on your pre-shot routine, as Marvin Sangüesa, a professional golfer and coach, emphasizes, can be a powerful technique to ward off distractions. This routine acts as a cue for your mind and body to shift into the task at hand. It's about preparing yourself both physically and mentally to perform the shot. This routine could involve anything from calculating your stroke and aligning your stance, to taking a few deep, calming breaths.

Visualization

Visualizing your shots before executing them is another significant part of honing focus. Visualization is a method used by athletes worldwide, picturing in their mind's eye exactly how they want their performance to go. This mental rehearsal primes your brain for success and can boost confidence.

Now, take a moment to reflect. When you're on the green, preparing to hit the ball, where does your mind wander? Are you solely concentrating on the ball, or are thoughts about past mistakes and future concerns creeping in? The key to success lies in taming these conscious and subconscious images. The conscious image is the active visualization of your desired shot, the trajectory, and the landing spot. The subconscious image, however, can be more elusive. It's the undercurrent of thoughts, the silent whisperings of self-doubt or over-confidence, that can undermine your play. Distinguishing between these two and maintaining a balance can be crucial to your success in golf.

Experts like Julie Wells suggest techniques to regain focus when it starts to wane. It could be a ritual like grabbing a new golf ball or humming your favorite tune. Experts highlight the importance of being aware of your internal chatter, which can often lead to tension and inconsistent performance. Being cognizant of your self-talk can aid you in mitigating any negative impacts on your game.

The common thread in all this advice is the power of the mind. The key lies in understanding that focus is not a constant state. It fluctuates, and that's normal. As Kristin Walla, a renowned golf strategist says, the goal is not to prevent the thoughts but to let them float away, replacing them with positive and specific ones.

The golf course is an arena of external factors that are out of your control. Your reaction to these factors, however, is within your control. And that's where your focus should be.

Pinpoint Precision

In golf, as in life, precision is the cornerstone of success. But in golf, precision isn't just about where you want the ball to go. It extends to the mental realm as well, shaping where your focus rests, honing your thoughts, and ultimately influencing your performance on the course.

Pinpoint precision in golf is twofold, involving both physical and mental aspects. Physically, it's about the calculated swings, the meticulous alignment, and the measured force behind each stroke. Mentally, however, it's about the deliberate focus, the tuned-in attention, and the intentionality behind every thought. An important concept to grasp is the idea of "focusing on your focus." It might sound redundant, but this self-aware approach to concentration is paramount. It's about becoming aware of your attention—where it is directed, how it drifts, and when it needs to be reined in. It's about exercising control over your thought patterns and maintaining a steadfast mental presence that complements your physical one.

Go Inward

Go inward, and narrow your focus. The world around you is full of distractions, all competing for a slice of your attention. The chirping of birds, the whispers of the wind, the rustling of leaves—while these sounds might be part of the game's charm, they can also deter your concentration. Here's where the importance of honing your focus comes in. Tune into your mind, observe your thoughts without judgment, and steer your focus toward what is within your control: your attitude, your preparation, and your response to challenges.

Focusing When the Time is Right

The art of concentration in golf isn't about being focused all the time; instead, it's about focusing when the time is right. Golf is a marathon, not a sprint, and maintaining a high level of concentration throughout the entire round can be both exhausting and counterproductive. Instead, it's more effective to focus on specific windows of time, like when you're preparing for a shot or analyzing the terrain. Between these instances, allow your mind to relax, unwind and recharge.

Take note of PGA professional Kellie Stenzel's advice of having a trigger to start your focus. This could be a gesture, a phrase, or an object—anything that signals to your mind that it's time to switch on the focus. Once the task is completed, allow yourself to switch off, conserve your mental energy, and prepare for the next round of concentration.

In a game of golf, the journey between the tee and the hole is filled with lessons on focus, precision, and control. It's a microcosm of life's larger picture where the journey matters just as much as the destination, and the secret to success lies in balancing the external world with the internal one. So, the next time you step onto the green, remember: it's not about just directing the ball, but also about guiding your mind. Keep your focus sharp, your control steadfast, and let the game play out, one mindful stroke at a time.

Staying Focused in Golf

In the grand theater of the green, every golfer has a unique script to follow. Amid the beautiful backdrops and intense competitive spirit, golf is a mental game that demands laser-sharp focus. In this intricate dance between the club and the ball, let's explore some methods to improve focus and performance.

Dealing With Distractions

The ability to keep distractions at bay is pivotal to staying focused in golf. These could be external distractions, such as environmental conditions, or internal distractions, like thoughts and emotions. Preparation is the key. Familiarize yourself with the course, understand its ins and outs, and take a few practice shots to warm up. This can act as a distraction-proof armor when you step on the turf.

Sometimes, the buzz of busier courses can disrupt concentration. In such situations, opt for quieter spots or off-peak times to sharpen your skills. Remember, though, golf is played under varying conditions, and the ability to balance between quieter and busier courses can be an ace up your sleeve.

The Importance of Mental Breaks

Golf requires a tremendous amount of mental energy. Therefore, it's essential to punctuate your round with regular mental breaks. These breaks provide an opportunity to recharge, regroup, and refocus. Walk around, stretch your muscles, hydrate, and indulge in deep breathing exercises.

Consider your golf round as a marathon, not a sprint. Segregating it into manageable chunks allows your mind to rest and refuel for the demanding holes. As the old golfing wisdom says, "The real game begins at the back nine;" taking mental breaks helps you stay focused and finish strong.

Deliberate Practice off the Course

Time spent away from the course is equally impactful to your performance on it. When practicing off the course, remember, quality trumps quantity. It's not about hitting a hundred balls aimlessly; it's about hitting thirty-five with intention and focus. The mantra is to be deliberate in your practice, focusing on the minute intricacies of your game.

Golf is a game of patience, and rushing your shots might lead to errors. Take your time, perfect your technique, and ensure accuracy in every shot. Embrace the rhythm of the game, and let the harmony reflect in your performance.

The Power of Routines

A routine is like an anchor, providing stability in the choppy sea of uncertainties that golf can sometimes be. A good pre-shot routine can create a sense of familiarity, setting the tone for your shot. But don't stop there. Create a post-shot routine as well.

Golf is a roller-coaster ride of great and not-so-great shots. Maintaining an even keel is crucial. After a shot, whether it's a hole-in-one or a swing-and-a-miss, hit the mental reset button. This could be as simple as taking a few deep breaths or repeating a positive affirmation.

Setting Personal Boundaries

Respect for the game also extends to your golfing partners. It's essential to set boundaries around how you approach the game. Communicate these to your playing partners to ensure that they understand and respect your focus on the game. Maintaining a sense of fair play and consideration is also crucial. If a partner is struggling, offer support rather than exploiting their weakness. Golf is a gentleman's or gentlewoman's game, and displaying etiquette is as significant as keeping your eye on the ball.

Remember, golf is a journey, not a destination. It's about those priceless moments of learning, self-improvement, and joy. It's about staying focused, not just on the ball, but also on the bigger picture—the love for the game. So, embrace these tips, improve your focus, and let the game of golf unfold its magic on you.

The Three Types of Focus in Golf

In the realm of sports, focus is a critical component in achieving success. This holds particularly true in golf, where your attention can drastically alter the outcome of your swing. Here, we will delve into the three types of focus: internal, external, and neutral, and how each can be beneficially applied to the game of golf.

Internal Focus

An internal focus centers on the mechanics of the golf swing itself. It entails a deep awareness of your body's movements, like how your wrists flex during the swing or the rotation of your shoulders. It's similar to dissecting a dance sequence into smaller, individual moves.

For instance, you might focus on how your hands grip the club, how your legs maintain balance, or how your shoulders rotate during the swing. However, similar to the way too much scrutiny might make even walking feel awkward, an excessive internal focus can disrupt the natural flow of your golf swing. However, in certain situations, like when you're learning a new technique or trying to correct a flaw in your swing, an internal focus can be beneficial. It's like learning a new dance routine; you have to pay attention to each step until it becomes second nature.

External Focus

An external focus, on the other hand, involves concentrating on elements outside your body. Rather than focusing on your swing's mechanics, you direct your attention to the impact of your swing on the ball, the ball's trajectory, or the intended target.

Let's consider a young golfer attempting to avoid bunkers on the golf course. By placing their focus on the task of keeping the ball away from the sand, they may naturally adjust their swing or stance, steering clear of the hazards without actively focusing on changing their swing. The beauty of an external focus is that it allows you to "let go," enabling your body to naturally adjust to achieve the desired outcome. It frees you from overthinking the technicalities, often resulting in an improvement in performance.

Neutral Focus

A neutral focus is a different beast altogether. This form of attention doesn't involve your swing or the flight of the ball. Instead, you're focusing on something unrelated to the golf game, such as the rhythm of your breathing or a catchy tune stuck in your head. Think of a teenage golfer about to make a crucial putt under pressure. By focusing on the melody of their favorite song, they can keep their nerves in check, preventing them from freezing up. The act of humming the song provides a form of mental escape, allowing them to execute the putt smoothly.

Neutral focus can be particularly useful in high-pressure situations or for those struggling with performance anxiety. It's a mental strategy that can help to soothe nerves, promoting a sense of calm and allowing players to execute their shots with a clear mind.

Using Each Focus Type to Your Advantage

Each type of focus has its unique benefits, and knowing when to employ each can significantly improve your game. An internal focus is especially handy when you're learning new skills or making adjustments to your swing. It can provide a clearer understanding of your swing's mechanics, but be wary of over-focusing on these aspects during play. Too much internal focus can lead to over-analysis, inhibiting the natural flow of your swing.

An external focus, on the other hand, is beneficial during actual gameplay. It shifts your attention away from your body to the task at hand, enabling your body to adjust naturally and accomplish the desired results. It's about playing the game, not just the swing.

A neutral focus can be the wildcard of your mental toolkit. It's not about the swing or the outcome but about achieving a mental state that allows your body to perform what it has been trained to do.

Stories to Inspire: Reading With the TV On

In our daily life, distractions can be both an adversary and an ally. They are usually perceived as an enemy when we are trying to accomplish a task or achieve a goal, while at other times, they can provide a much-needed break from monotony or intense concentration. But imagine harnessing distractions to your benefit to enhance your focus and performance rather than hinder it. Sounds unconventional? This rather unconventional notion originates from none other than Tiger

Woods, widely regarded as one of the most exceptional golfers in history.

From his early years, Woods has been conditioned to perform under immense pressure, dealing with distractions like heckling from his father and massive expectations from the world. His journey to becoming the greatest golfer of his generation was a blend of innate talent, rigorous training, and an exceptional mental strategy. One of the key mental lessons Woods shared with fellow golfer Harold Varner III is one that we can all learn from. Varner recalled asking Woods how he maintains his focus during games amidst the inevitable cacophony of crowd noise, to which Woods replied, "Playing golf is like reading a book with the TV on."

This metaphor is simple yet profound. Woods isn't advocating for shutting out the world around us when we need to concentrate. Instead, he encourages us to embrace our surroundings, even when they're filled with distractions. The aim isn't to ignore the noise but to become comfortable with it, to acknowledge it without letting it derail us from our objectives.

Woods's approach, though it might seem counterintuitive initially, holds immense wisdom. It encourages us to adapt to and exist within the noise, distractions, and pressures rather than trying to eliminate or avoid them. After all, in real life, we don't always have the luxury of silence or solitude when we need to focus.

In response to Woods's advice, Varner practiced his focus by reading with the television on, attempting to hone his concentration amidst the distraction. This simple yet effective strategy can be utilized by us all. It teaches us to control our attention, to focus amidst the chaos, and to stay on track even when our environment seems designed to distract us.

So, the next time you find yourself in a distracting environment, remember Woods's advice. Instead of getting frustrated or trying to block everything out, make peace with the distractions and learn to function within them. This way, you can turn the challenge of a noisy world into a strength, a tool to enhance your concentration and performance. It's a story to inspire, a lesson from the golf course that can be applied to many aspects of our lives, from studying for a test to performing under pressure or even simply reading a book with the TV on.

Teeing Up: Actionable Steps to Improve Focus

We've explored the crucial role of focus in golf and how it can be enhanced to improve your game. Now, let's turn these insights into practical steps that can be put into action to develop your concentration skills on the golf course. We will divide these strategies into two sections: one for the coach and one for the athlete. Let's start teeing up!

For the Coach

1. Cultivate the right mindset: Remind your athletes that golf is more about playing against the course than against the opponents. Encourage them to focus on their game and not get distracted by the performance of others.

2. Guide the focus: Teach your athletes what to concentrate on and what to tune out. Explain the significance of focusing on elements within their control and guide them to develop their visualization skills.

3. Introduce focus exercises: Incorporate focus exercises into practice sessions. This can involve mindfulness techniques

or practical exercises like hitting a target from different distances.

4. Promote balanced focus: Help your athletes understand the three types of focus (internal, external, and neutral) and when to utilize each for optimal performance.

5. Manage off-course influences: Encourage your athletes to maintain their mental health outside of golf. Stress that a calm and focused mind off the course will translate into a better focus on the course.

For the Athlete

1. Embrace the right perspective: Remember that your real competition is the golf course, not necessarily other players. Concentrate on your game, your strategy, and your technique.

2. Master the art of tuning in and out: Train yourself to focus on the important aspects of your game while filtering out distractions. Practice visualization techniques to enhance your concentration skills.

3. Adopt a process-focused approach: Avoid focusing solely on outcomes. Instead, pay attention to your process and the steps you're taking to execute each shot.

4. Utilize different focus strategies: Understand and practice using internal, external, and neutral focus to boost your performance in different situations on the golf course.

5. Manage your off-course mental health: Look after your mental well-being outside of golf. Recognize that good men-

tal health contributes to better focus and, ultimately, better performance on the course.

Remember that focus, like any other skill in golf, requires practice and patience. Implement these steps consistently, and, with time, you'll see a noticeable improvement in your ability to stay on course and maintain a winning edge.

Conclusion

Chapter 2 underscores the significance of setting personal boundaries and maintaining respect in the game of golf. It highlights that golf is not just about the individual player but also about being considerate and supportive toward others, thus embodying the true spirit of this prestigious game. The chapter advocates for a holistic approach to golf, seeing it as a journey of self-improvement, learning, and joy.

In the next chapter, the emphasis will be on the importance of emotional control, a critical mental toughness skill. Just as setting personal boundaries is crucial for respectful interaction with others on the golf course, maintaining emotional control is key for managing one's own gameplay. By controlling one's emotions, a golfer can better navigate the highs and lows of the game, ultimately leading to improved focus and performance. This skill complements the values of respect and consideration discussed in Chapter 2 and is a critical component of mental toughness in golf.

Chapter 3: Skill #2-Emotional Mastery

The sun was breaking over the horizon as a distinctly Scottish brogue filled the cool morning air: "I'm trying not to get too emotional [on the course]; whatever happens, just hit it, deal with it, hit it again." Robert MacIntyre, one of the game's most promising talents, was sharing his nuggets of wisdom with an air of composed confidence. From the highlands of Scotland to the lush greens of Augusta, he carries these words with him, a personal mantra that exemplifies the emotional strength required on the golf course.

MacIntyre, hailing from Oban, a coastal town that's more famous for its whisky than its golfers, is a testament to emotional fortitude in the face of adversity. His journey is one marked by perseverance, emotional control, and an unwavering determination that underlines the ethos of this chapter: mastering your emotions to refine your game. He understands that the battle on the golf course is not merely against the elements or the challenging course design; it's also a battle within oneself.

Another golfing legend, Bobby Jones, once said, "Golf is a game that is played on a five-inch course—the distance between your ears." It's this internal struggle, the tempest of emotions that swirl in these crucial five inches, which often determines victory or defeat. It's the pivotal moment when frustration from a miscalculated swing or the anxiety of a crucial putt can lead to the dreaded "Bogey Train," a chain of poor shots driven by a snowballing negative mindset.

It's all too common to witness players who turn into Smashers, Throwers, or Yellers under the immense pressure of the game wasting precious energy, not on their game, but on their unrestrained emotional outbursts. They often become ensnared in the internal struggle between the emotional brain and the thinking brain, where the primal fight-or-flight response often overshadows conscious thought. It's in these critical moments that the skill of emotional mastery becomes indispensable.

But where do these tumultuous emotions stem from? Perfectionism? Fear of failure? Unrealistic expectations? Often, it's a combination of these factors, coupled with personal life stressors and physical health. The fear of choking, tied tightly to perfectionism, and the expectations we set can be paralyzing. However, being aware of these sources can help us combat them effectively, providing the mental clarity needed for peak performance.

Armed with the knowledge of where these emotions originate, the next step is managing them. By employing techniques such as detachment, acceptance, and focused refocusing, we can avoid becoming our worst enemies on the course. It's not about suppressing our feelings but rather about acknowledging them, giving them their due, and then redirecting our attention back to the game. It's about reminding ourselves that golf, like life, is about the process, not just the outcome. Building emotional strength and control is not an overnight endeavor. It's about cultivating a growth mindset, becoming aware of our triggers, and finding actionable ways to combat them. It's about giving yourself the permission to feel the emotion, letting it pass, and then refocusing on the next shot. Breathwork can play a crucial role here, not only to help us calm down but also to hone our mental strength.

Let's take a leaf out of pro golfer Brooks Koepka's book, who once said, "It's just a game. I'm trying to do the best I can. I work hard, and whatever happens, happens." He epitomizes the right approach toward a bad day on the course.

In the end, it's important to remember that although you may not have direct control over your emotions, you do possess the ability to govern your responses using your cognitive faculties. This is emotional mastery, the key to unlocking your true golfing potential. As we progress through this chapter, we will explore these themes in more detail, providing practical advice and actionable strategies that you can employ both on and off the course. We will help you transform your approach to the game, to not only become a better golfer but to become a more resilient person, as well.

Personal Principles of Robert MacIntyre

Scottish professional golfer Robert MacIntyre's success on the greens is a testament to his firm belief in emotional management. His philosophy is simple yet profound. MacIntyre's belief in keeping calm in the face of adversity is deeply ingrained in his personal philosophy. He grew up playing a variety of sports in addition to golf. The volatile weather and challenging courses of his home country taught him early on the importance of perseverance, patience, and emotional composure.

Rather than allowing frustration or excitement to cloud his judgment, MacIntyre prefers to view each shot as an isolated event. His approach is to accept whatever outcome occurs and move on to the next shot with a clear mind. This mindfulness allows him to focus on the task at hand, preventing the "snowball effect" of one poor shot leading to another. In golf, every stroke comes with its unique set of challenges and opportunities. MacIntyre believes that getting overly emotional, whether positively or negatively, can lead to rash decisions and hinder his performance. Instead, he stresses the importance of managing emotions and maintaining an even temperament. His focus is on the present moment, not the past or the future.

MacIntyre's personal principles extend beyond his own performance on the golf course. He firmly believes that these principles can be beneficial to golfers of all ages and levels of experience. From teenagers just beginning to learn the sport to adults playing in a local league, his message is the same: managing your emotions is critical to success in golf. And his approach seems to be working. As of 2023, MacIntyre has consistently ranked among the top golfers in the world, a testament to his discipline, skill, and unflappable emotional control. His philosophy serves as a reminder to golfers everywhere: your emotions can be powerful, but they need not control you. Instead, accept them, manage them, and focus on the shot at hand.

In a sport as mentally demanding as golf, Robert MacIntyre's approach provides a blueprint for emotional management. His triumph stands as a compelling testament to the potency of maintaining composure, embracing acceptance, and sustaining unwavering focus when confronted with challenges. Indeed, in the game of golf and in life, sometimes the optimal course of action involves identifying the issue, confronting it, and striking once more.

How Emotions Weaken Players

Emotions are the unseen forces that affect a player's performance in any sport, including golf. When negative emotions such as frustration, anger, or anxiety get the better of a golfer, they can undermine both the physical and mental aspects of their game. The swing, which is a complex combination of timing, coordination, and precision, can be disrupted by the physiological changes brought about by these emotions.

Take frustration, for instance. It is a common response to a missed shot or a poor decision on the course. This feeling can cause a golfer's muscles to tense, disrupt their focus, and prompt rushed decisions, all of which can lead to more mistakes, thus entering a vicious cycle. This phenomenon is often referred to as "The Bogey Train" or the snowball effect, where one bad shot leads to another and another, with the golfer's state of mind deteriorating with each error.

The golfer's general emotional state, too, has a significant impact on their swing and overall performance. Chronic anxiety or unresolved anger, for example, can lead to inconsistencies in the execution of the swing. If a golfer is feeling nervous or angry, their body may react in ways that alter the tempo of their swing, disrupt their focus, or prompt them to make poor decisions on the course. Emotions, therefore, have the power to affect not only a golfer's physical ability but also their mental acuity.

Waste of Energy

Investing emotional energy in negative thoughts and feelings is not only detrimental to performance but is also an ineffective use of a golfer's resources. It is energy that could be better used in focusing on the next shot, developing strategy, or simply enjoying the game. Acknowledging the emotion, breathing through it, feeling it, and then releasing it allows a golfer to process the emotion without letting it consume their focus or drain their energy.

Coping Strategies

Recognizing the impact of emotions on performance is the first step in managing them. Once a golfer acknowledges the power of their emotional state, they can begin to use strategies to cope with negative feelings. These might include deep breathing exercises, humor to alleviate tension, or mental exercises to shift focus away from past mistakes or future outcomes and keep attention on the present shot.

A critical part of coping with negative emotions is understanding that everyone, even professional golfers, experiences bouts of frustration, anxiety, or fear on the course. Mistakes are part of the game, and they are not "awful" unless they are allowed to snowball into more mistakes. Letting go of the idea that a mistake is a catastrophe can help a golfer remain composed, focus on the next shot, and ultimately get off the "bogey train."

Emotions can be a golf player's worst enemy or their greatest ally. By recognizing and managing them effectively, players can ensure that their emotional state enhances, rather than detracts from, their performance on the course.

Identifying Your Temperament

The realm of golf isn't simply confined to precision, swing, and technique; it also serves as an illuminating theater of emotions. Certain instances often unveil different shades of temperament, quite evident in the common archetypes of angry golfers. These personas paint the turf with their vibrant reactions, turning a serene golf course into a vivid canvas of expressions.

The Smasher

Let's start with the Smasher. This archetype channels their frustration into the ground, treating their club as a hammer of anger after a disappointing putt. With each stroke not living up to their expectation, the course shakes under their displeasure.

The Thrower

Then, there is the Thrower. When their ball lands in an unfavorable spot, say amongst the trees, they propel their driver through the air, transforming a peaceful atmosphere into an unintentional javelin field. Their clubs often find themselves soaring higher than their golf balls.

The Breaker

Next, we have the Breaker. The Breaker puts an untimely end to their club's life, bending it over their knee after a stray drive. They take the term "break the game" too literally, as if punishing their club would rectify the errant shots.

The Yeller

Lastly, we encounter the Yeller. They vocalize their discontent with every misaimed hit, whether it lands in a sand trap or beyond the intended target. Their cries echo across the greens, adding an unplanned soundtrack to the game. These manifestations of anger and frustration, however, do more harm than good. Unrestrained negative emotions can ripple across your body and mind, creating an unwelcome tension that distorts your focus and disrupts your game. But the silver lining is that these emotions don't have to be your downfall. Instead, they can be transformed into stepping stones toward becoming a better player.

Consider this a challenge and an opportunity to master your emotional response. Focus on the next move, keeping your mind in the present moment. See the next shot as a task at hand, and concentrate on putting yourself in the best position to play it. Simultaneously, cultivate a sense of relaxation, allowing your mind to declutter from intrusive negative thoughts and allowing your body to swing freely.

Inside Your Brain

In the game of golf and in other aspects of life, emotions play a significant role in influencing our performance. Emotions, either positive or negative, can affect our decision-making abilities, concentration, and overall performance. To explain what's happening inside our brain that causes these shifts, we have to understand the brain's structure and the roles of different parts of the brain in processing and controlling emotions. For this discussion, we will use the metaphor of the "alligator," representing the emotional brain, and the cognitive mind is symbolized by the term "computer."

Emotional Brain vs Thinking Brain

The thinking brain and the emotional brain are distinct components within our brain that serve unique functions. The emotional brain, often represented by the metaphorical alligator, is responsible for survival instincts and emotional responses. The thinking brain, represented by the metaphorical computer, is responsible for rational decision-making and logical reasoning.

Understanding How the Two Interact With Each Other

These two brain components constantly interact with and influence each other. While the emotional brain processes emotions and triggers responses, the thinking brain evaluates the significance of these emotions and decides on appropriate actions. The interplay between these two parts of the brain is crucial for managing emotions effectively.

Your Emotional Brain Can Hijack Your Thinking Brain

During certain circumstances, the emotional brain can overwhelm the thinking brain, resulting in what is commonly referred to as emotional hijacking. When the emotional brain, specifically the amygdala, perceives a threat, it can send the individual into a fight-or-flight response. This response is characterized by the release of stress hormones and can override conscious thought processes, impairing logical reasoning and decision-making abilities.

Behavior Cycle

There is a cyclical relationship between thoughts, emotions, and behaviors. Thoughts can influence emotions, as our interpretations and perceptions shape our emotional responses. Emotions, in turn, can affect actions, influencing how we respond to certain situations. These actions, in a feedback loop, can also influence our subsequent thoughts and emotions.

Thoughts Affect Emotions

Our thoughts and interpretations of events can have a direct impact on our emotional responses. Positive thoughts and optimistic interpretations tend to generate positive emotions, while negative thoughts can lead to negative emotions.

Emotions Affect Actions

Emotions play a significant role in determining our actions. When we experience intense emotions, such as anger or fear, they can influence our actions and reactions. For example, feeling frustrated after a bad shot in golf might lead to impulsive or uncontrolled behaviors.

Actions Affect Thoughts

Our behaviors and actions can also influence our thoughts. Engaging in certain actions or behaviors can reinforce certain thought patterns or beliefs. For example, consistently performing well in golf can boost confidence and contribute to positive thoughts about one's abilities.

Gaining a comprehensive understanding of the complex interplay between the thinking brain and the emotional brain is crucial, allowing individuals to develop strategies for managing their emotions effectively and improving their overall performance and well-being.

Where do Emotions Come From?

Emotions are a complex and multi-dimensional aspect of the human experience. They stem from a combination of factors, including our physical state, mental state, environment, and experiences. In the context of golfers and golfing, these factors become even more intertwined, as the sport demands both physical skill and mental fortitude.

Life in General

Life, in general, is full of ups and downs, and these fluctuations naturally influence our emotional state. In golf, these emotions are often magnified due to the competitive and solitary nature of the sport. A golfer might feel joy after a well-executed swing, disappointment after a missed putt, or frustration when their performance is not up to their expectations. These emotions are tied to various aspects of their life, including personal expectations, desire for perfection, physical well-being, and fear of failure or disappointment.

Expectations

Expectations on the outcome are a significant source of emotions in golf. A golfer might have high hopes for a tournament, putting pressure on themselves to achieve a particular score or ranking. These expectations can lead to intense feelings of anticipation, excitement, anxiety, and disappointment. They can also result in stress and tension, which can physically impact a golfer's performance by causing tight muscles and disrupted focus.

Perfectionism

Perfectionism is another strong emotional driver in golf. Many golfers strive for a flawless performance, aiming to make each swing, drive, and putt with precision. The pursuit of perfection can lead to feelings of satisfaction and achievement when goals are met but can also generate frustration, self-doubt, and disappointment when they're not. It's essential to balance this striving for perfection with a realistic understanding that mistakes and off-days are part of the process and can provide valuable learning experiences.

Physical Health

Physical health plays a significant role in our emotional state. For golfers, this is even more pertinent, as their physical condition directly impacts their game. Pain and fatigue can lead to feelings of frustration, discouragement, and irritability, impacting not only their performance but also their enjoyment of the game. On the other hand, maintaining a healthy diet and balanced body chemistry can lead to improved mood, energy levels, and overall emotional well-being.

Fear

Fear is a particularly potent emotion in golf. This could be fear of underperformance, fear of not meeting expectations, or fear of physical pain or injury. Golfers may also fear choking under pressure, particularly in high-stakes games or tournaments. This fear can lead to increased stress levels, which can negatively affect a golfer's physical performance and mental focus. Fear is a pervasive emotion that can significantly influence a golfer's performance on the course. It's a natural human response designed to alert us to potential threats. However, in the context of golf, it can often serve as a mental roadblock, inhibiting performance and undermining confidence.

Fear of Choking

One common manifestation of fear in golf is the fear of choking, which refers to a situation where a golfer underperforms due to increased pressure or stress. This fear can stem from a variety of sources, such as high-stakes tournaments, challenging courses, or critical shots. Choking is often a self-fulfilling prophecy: the more a golfer fears it, the more likely it is to occur.

This fear of choking ties back to perfectionism and the kinds of expectations a golfer sets for themselves. Golfers who strive for perfection and have high expectations can place immense pressure on themselves, increasing their susceptibility to fear and potential for choking. In contrast, adopting a more balanced perspective that accepts occasional mistakes as part of the learning and growth process can help reduce the intensity of fear and the likelihood of choking.

Addressing this fear requires a combination of mental and emotional strategies. A key approach is to shift the focus from outcome-oriented thinking to process-oriented thinking. Instead of fixating on the potential for failure or a less-than-perfect outcome, golfers should focus on the elements within their control, such as their swing mechanics, breathing, and mental routine. Another effective strategy is to practice mindfulness and relaxation techniques. These can help golfers stay present in the moment, reducing anxiety and the fear of choking. By grounding themselves in the present, golfers can better manage their fear and prevent it from undermining their performance.

Remember that your mindset off the course can significantly impact how you feel on the course. If you're experiencing high levels of stress in other areas of your life, it's likely to carry over to your golf game, potentially increasing your fear and susceptibility to choking. Conversely, maintaining a balanced and positive mindset in life, in general, can translate into greater emotional stability and confidence on the golf course.

Maintaining a healthy lifestyle, cultivating positive relationships, engaging in stress-reducing activities, and seeking professional help when needed can all contribute to a healthier mindset. This positive mindset can then enhance your emotional resilience, reduce fear, and improve your overall performance and enjoyment of golf. Remember, golf is as much a mental game as it is a physical one, and taking care of your mental health is just as crucial as honing your physical skills.

The Art of Controlling Emotions in Golf

George Mumford, a mindfulness guru, once said, "Being your best means creating a space between stimulus and response, and in that space, you have the freedom and power to choose a response that aligns with your values and goals." This insightful notion forms the essence of what we'll discuss in this section: understanding and controlling emotions in golf. First, it's crucial to understand that emotions, thoughts, and behaviors are interconnected in an intricate loop. For example, in golf, an emotion of anxiety may spawn feelings of fear or doubt, which in turn trigger negative thoughts like, "I'm going to miss this putt," amplifying the initial anxiety and adversely affecting your play. The key to breaking this vicious cycle is the practice of mindfulness or self-awareness.

Mindfulness: The Secret Ingredient

Mindfulness helps you acknowledge thoughts, feelings, and emotions without letting them overwhelm you. It allows you to redirect your focus toward your values and intentions, silence the clamor of mental chatter, and accept your experiences. This acceptance cultivates emotional agility, allowing you to navigate through the challenges of the golf course with grace and ease.

Navigating the Emotional Landscape

When you feel the onset of an emotion, say, anxiety or anger, acknowledge it by saying to yourself, "I feel anxious" or "I feel angry."

This act of acceptance and self-compassion is the first step to gaining control over your emotions. It's important to remember that feelings are transient, not permanent. By noticing and accepting them, you create an emotional distance that allows these feelings to dissipate.

Once you acknowledge your emotions, try to identify their source. Often, these feelings have little to do with your current performance and more to do with external triggers or past experiences. Understanding the source can help neutralize the emotional impact and prevent it from skewing your perception and performance.

Controlling Emotions: A Step-by-step Approach

1. Acknowledge: Ask yourself, "What am I thinking, and how am I feeling now?" Be curious, not judgmental.

2. Accept: Say, "I'm thinking ____ and feeling _____, and that's okay."

3. Identify: Why do I feel that emotion?

4. Reset: Bring yourself back to the present moment by focusing on your breathing, smiling, or saying a positive affirmation.

Realign and Refocus

Once you've acknowledged, accepted, and identified your feelings, it's time to realign and refocus. Redirect your attention to the next shot, remember the overall process, and re-examine your expectations.

Remember, your focus should be on the process, not the outcome. When standing on the tee, it is important to avoid the mindset of "I must birdie this hole" to prevent setting oneself up for potential disappointment. Instead, focus on establishing a reliable pre-shot routine and adhere to it consistently. This method promotes consistency and aids in preventing distracting thoughts from interfering. Moreover, it's essential to keep your expectations reasonable and to give yourself the grace to fall short. If you set extremely high standards for yourself, you'll inevitably face disappointment when you come up short. Assess your skills honestly, set your goals accordingly, and always keep in mind that golf is ultimately a game—it is perfectly acceptable to make mistakes along the way.

In the end, remember that golf is not just about perfect shots or winning matches. It's about the journey, the experience, and the joy of playing. Remember, golf is just a game, and there are plenty of people who'd love to be in your shoes, enjoying a beautiful day on the green. When emotions threaten to get the best of you, take a deep breath, smile, and swing. Your game will thank you.

Building Emotional Strength and Control

For many golfers, from fledgling amateurs to seasoned pros, the emotional rollercoaster of golf can be as challenging as the physical gameplay. Emotion management and control are critical components to consistent golf performance, and much like a golfer's physical skills, they must be practiced and strengthened. So, let's delve into how one can build emotional strength, maintain stability, and foster a growth mindset to enhance their golf game.

To begin, imagine your favorite professional golfer. Broadcasters often highlight the importance of emotional control: If Rory, Rickie, Stacey, or Inbee can keep their emotions in check today, they have a chance to win this event. The same goes for us. If we fail to control our emotions, our game will suffer. This reality became a significant hurdle in my professional golf career, as negative emotions often sent me spiraling, hindering my focus and impacting my performance.

Let's establish this: Golf is not just a physical game—it's an emotional one. Understanding and managing your emotions might just be your most significant advantage on the course. This emotional challenge is heightened due to three factors: you're alone with no teammates to lean on; there's a substantial amount of time between shots for overthinking; and stress hormones like adrenaline and cortisol, which may enhance performance in certain sports, do not necessarily provide an advantage in golf.

Building Your Emotional Muscles

To better manage your emotions and improve your game, start by building your emotional muscles. Much like physical training, developing emotional strength takes practice and persistence. However, once developed, these "muscles" will allow you to better leverage your talent, work, and efforts. Just like a physical muscle, you can train and develop your emotional muscle. Here's how:

1. Self-Awareness and Tracking Your Triggers: Gain a comprehensive understanding of your strengths, limitations, and triggers. Identify your areas of expertise, recognize the aspects that pose challenges, and become aware of the specific circumstances that elicit negative reactions. Awareness can help you avoid reacting impulsively and help you make better decisions on the golf course.

2. 90-Second Rule: When emotions spike, apply the 90-second rule. Neuroscience research shows that an emotional reaction lasts about 90 seconds from the initial trigger. When you sense an emotion intensifying, take a deep breath, and allow it approximately 90 seconds to naturally subside. By doing so, you can effectively manage and alleviate your emotions, preventing them from adversely affecting your performance.

3. Staying Present: The past and future can distract and stir emotions. Concentrate on the present moment. Your destiny resides in the present moment. While your goals are rooted in the future, they are attained by fully engaging in and embracing the present.

4. Breathwork: This is an excellent tool for calming your nerves and honing mental strength. Deep, intentional breathing helps maintain emotional stability, improves focus, and enhances overall performance.

Building emotional strength takes time and practice. Nevertheless, attaining mastery over emotional control has the power to unlock your full potential and elevate your golf game to new heights. Remember, the key to a successful golf career isn't just physical skill—it's also about emotional strength and control, so start building your emotional muscles today.

Stories to Inspire: When Bad Days Happen—The Tale of Brooks Koepka

Golf is a game that mirrors life itself: unpredictable, challenging, sometimes downright frustrating, but above all, exhilarating. It's a sport that demands not only physical precision but also immense mental fortitude. Let's take a look at the inspiring story of Brooks Koepka and how he copes when even the surest victory takes an unexpected turn toward defeat.

Brooks Koepka is one of the most acclaimed golfers of his generation, renowned for his physical prowess, unwavering confidence, and ironclad mental toughness. But what truly sets him apart is his extraordinary ability to navigate the tumultuous waters of defeat. A particular instance that comes to mind is the Masters at Augusta National, a day that stands as a testament to his resilience. The setting was nothing short of picture-perfect. Brooks had been playing phenomenally, making putts, hitting fairways and greens with precision. His victory at the LIV Golf event prior to Augusta had boosted his confidence, and he arrived at Augusta National with a sense of momentum that was palpable. Heading into the ultimate round of the Masters, he maintained a two-shot lead over his fellow player, the Spaniard Jon Rahm.

But golf, much like life, is a fickle game. Despite his stellar performance leading up to the final round, Brooks fell short of claiming his first green jacket. His usually impeccable game seemed just a touch off, resulting in a final round score of 3 over par, 75. Meanwhile, Jon Rahm slipped on his first green jacket, having turned his initial setback, a double bogey on the first hole, into an eagle on his very next hole.

Defeat can be a bitter pill to swallow, especially when victory seems well within grasp. But here's where the true measure of Brooks's mental toughness came to the fore. Despite his disappointment, Brooks was gracious in defeat. "I tried my hardest, gave it my all," he remarked during his post-round press conference, displaying an incredible sense of resilience and humility.

Brooks's approach to bad days is one of acceptance and optimism. He understands that bad rounds can follow good ones, and that a single unlucky swing or an unexpected turn can drastically alter the course of the game. But instead of dwelling on what went wrong, he focuses on giving his best effort every single time. His philosophy revolves around the concept of resilience. No matter how tough the round or how high the stakes, he remains steadfast in his commitment to give his all, unafraid to risk failure in pursuit of success. This is the mindset that every aspiring golfer, indeed every teenager, should seek to emulate. Brooks Koepka teaches us that no setback, however disheartening, should ever prevent us from laying it all on the line and trying our best.

In the grand scheme of things, your score is just a number. What truly matters is the process, the lessons learned along the way, and having the strength to bounce back when the going gets tough. As Brooks Koepka's story vividly illustrates, bad days are inevitable. But how we handle those bad days, how we respond to failure, is what truly defines us. Brooks's inspiring journey is a testament to the power of resilience and mental fortitude. When bad days happen—as they inevitably will—remember his story. Use it as a reminder to never let setbacks deter you from your path, to always give your all, and, most importantly, to be gracious, whether in victory or defeat.

Teeing Up: Actionable Steps to Master Your Emotions

This chapter delved into the role of emotions in golf and how they can be harnessed to improve performance. Now it's time to translate these insights into concrete steps that can be taken to enhance emotional management on the golf course. We'll split these steps into two sections: one for the coach and one for the athlete.

For the Coach

1. Educate about the Impact of Emotions: Teach your athletes about the influence of emotions on performance. Make them aware of the potential pitfalls of emotions like frustration and the "snowball effect."

2. Identify Emotional Triggers: Help your athletes identify

their emotional triggers. Encourage them to track their emotional responses during games and practice sessions to understand what might provoke emotional responses.

3. Promote Self-Awareness: Encourage athletes to be mindful of their emotions and their sources. Foster an environment where they can openly discuss their feelings without judgment.

4. Teach Emotional Control Techniques: Introduce techniques for managing negative emotions, such as the 90-second rule, deep breathing exercises, and the practice of acceptance.

5. Encourage a Growth Mindset: Foster a growth mindset among your athletes. Remind them that every challenge, mistake, or setback is an opportunity for learning and improvement.

For the Athlete

1. Understand Your Emotions: Learn about the impact of emotions on your performance. Understand how negative emotions can lead to poor performance and identify the typical emotional responses that hinder your play.

2. Track Your Emotional Triggers: Keep a record of instances when you become emotionally overwhelmed during a game. By understanding your triggers, you can work on strategies to manage these situations better.

3. Practice Emotional Control Techniques: Use the 90-second rule to let your emotions pass, practice deep breathing exer-

cises, and learn to accept your feelings without judgment.

4. Adopt a Growth Mindset: See every challenge as an opportunity to learn and improve. Avoid fixating on your errors; instead, redirect your attention toward extracting valuable lessons from them.

5. Work on Your Emotional Strength: Develop strategies to strengthen your emotional control. This could be through maintaining a mental scorecard, focusing on the process rather than the outcome, or by re-evaluating your expectations.

Remember, emotional mastery, like any other skill in golf, requires consistent practice and effort. As you begin to implement these steps, you'll gradually notice improvements in your ability to manage your emotions on the golf course, leading to better overall performance.

Conclusion

Emotional mastery is pivotal to enhancing golf performance. This chapter outlined how unchecked emotions can hinder performance, leading to a cycle of poor play. We examined the origins of these emotions and suggested effective strategies for managing them, using the examples of renowned golfers Robert MacIntyre and Brooks Koepka. As we forge ahead, embrace the principles discussed and look forward to the next chapter that delves into the significance of discipline and routine in golf.

Chapter 4: Skill #3–Do the Disciplines

"There is beauty in tomorrow," the legendary golfer Tiger Woods once declared. "The greatest thing about tomorrow is I will be better than I am today. That's how I look at my life... That's the beauty of tomorrow." But what does it mean to be better tomorrow? Is it merely a promise for the dawn or a concept that is wielded, like a well-balanced golf club, with precision, discipline, and an enduring commitment to the mastery of one's craft? In this chapter, we explore the heart of Woods' philosophy, illuminating the intricate dance between time management, discipline, and mental toughness.

Woods, known as much for his mental strength as for his physical prowess, wielded discipline like a finely honed tool, chiseling his victories in the face of fierce competition and personal challenges. His mantra of being better tomorrow wasn't simply a reference to improved swing or putting accuracy; it was a testament to the power of discipline and the relentless pursuit of mental toughness.

Imagine a golfer on a practice range. The sun is setting, casting long shadows across the field. The golfer has a bag of balls at his side. He picks one up, positions it, steps back, swings, and watches as it soars. Then he repeats the process. Over and over again, each movement deliberate, each decision calculated. This routine isn't merely an act of practice; it's a testament to discipline. It's a matter of understanding that excellence, just like your swing, can't be improved without disciplined practice. However, the path of discipline is not a well-trodden trail, especially for younger golfers. Imagine being at the casino. Most golfers, particularly the younger ones, are gamblers—hoping to hit the jackpot with one lucky swing, one lucky game. Yet, discipline calls for us to be the casino, instead—consistent, strategic, understanding that small decisions, done consistently, lead to achieving big goals. This approach requires a shift in perspective, a willingness to embrace the mundane and repetitive in pursuit of greatness.

Yet, how does one cultivate this discipline? Picture yourself preparing for a shot. You take your stance, focus your gaze on the ball, and at that moment, nothing else matters. The crowd fades into the background; your opponent becomes a blur in your peripheral vision. This is discipline, a marriage of focus and consistency, a mental frame that holds steady, directing your mind and body toward your goal.

And so, with each repetition, with each disciplined thought and action, you are embedding routines, replacing old habits with better ones. A routine encompasses more than a mere series of actions; it represents a purposeful sequence, a meticulously choreographed set of precise movements that, when executed consistently, evolves into a defining characteristic of your playing style.

There are tales of golfers whose disciplined approach has led them to remarkable success. Consider the story of Jon Rahm, who, through discipline, learned to combine his raw talent with emotional self-control. His journey highlights the transformative power of discipline in channeling one's emotions and skills to ascend to the pinnacle of the game.

In the sections that follow, we will delve into these concepts further, exploring the intricacies of discipline, how it is intertwined with mental toughness, and how it shapes the journey from the practice range to the Master's green. This is our exploration of the beauty of tomorrow—a disciplined journey toward a better self.

What Is the Deal With Discipline?

The deal with discipline is not as ominous as it sounds; rather, it's a fundamental aspect that ties together success and progress in numerous aspects of life, including golf. Discipline, in the most basic sense, is the practice of training oneself to follow a particular code of behavior or conduct. It involves consistency, dedication, and commitment to a specific routine or set of tasks. In golf, discipline translates into a routine of consistent actions, practices, or behaviors. This consistency is key in executing a successful shot, a well-aimed putt, or even a perfectly timed swing. In essence, it is the ability to repeat the same tasks in the same order, time and time again, and do so effectively.

Making Things Routine

The idea of discipline creating routine is a critical factor in its importance. Routines become familiar, comfortable, and something we can trust to produce reliable outcomes. For example, when we wake up in the morning, we often have a set routine that we follow, and it becomes automatic. The same principle applies to golf. By establishing a disciplined routine in the game, like a pre-shot routine, we allow ourselves to think less, trust more, and execute actions with increased ease and confidence.

Creating discipline in your golf game essentially requires a dedicated approach to practice, the willingness to learn, and the ability to eliminate distractions. The pre-shot routine, an ordered set of tasks completed before every shot, serves as a great example of discipline in golf. It's a consistent process that prepares you mentally and physically for the shot ahead. If repeated consistently, it can foster a sense of predictability and control, enhancing your overall performance.

A disciplined pre-shot routine could include assessing the environment, selecting the right club, visualizing the shot, aligning the shot, taking practice swings, and finally, executing the shot. This routine, repeated consistently, leads to familiarity and confidence, offering the best chance for a successful shot. Being disciplined doesn't just apply to the game of golf; it's a valuable life skill that applies to many aspects of our lives. From studying for tests to pursuing a fitness goal, the concept of discipline, of repeating a certain set of tasks in a specific order and making it a routine, contributes to the likelihood of achieving desired outcomes.

Discipline is not about punishment or restriction; rather, it's about fostering consistency, reliability, and, ultimately, success. By embracing discipline, whether on the golf course or in life, we set ourselves up for a pathway that leads to increased proficiency, competence, and achievement. Remember, in the grand scheme of things, it's not just about hitting the perfect shot, but it's also about embracing the journey that leads to it—a journey framed by the well-placed strokes of discipline.

Importance of Discipline in Golf

Discipline in golf extends far beyond merely showing up to the driving range for practice sessions. It is an integral aspect of developing mental toughness, which is a crucial attribute not just in sports but in all facets of life. In golf, as in life, mental toughness determines the difference between mere participants and true achievers. For the young golfers and their parents reading this, understanding the importance of discipline is the first step to a journey that could mold your game and your life. Golf, as a sport, has a unique ability to teach discipline due to its solitary nature. It's just the player, the club, and the ball. There's no teammate to pass to or coach to rely on during play. In these quiet moments, players learn to manage their thoughts and emotions, leading to heightened mental toughness. Discipline in golf is not just about physical consistency but about the mental fortitude required to keep going, even when the odds seem insurmountable.

For young golfers, discipline is the catalyst that allows them to rise above their current skill level. A golfer could have a perfect swing, but without the discipline to maintain focus, adapt to changing conditions, and continually strive for improvement, that swing is not worth much. Discipline fuels the drive to identify and work on weaknesses. It's the force that prompts players to work on their short game when they'd rather be driving balls or spend time practicing tricky shots when they could be cruising through easier rounds.

Discipline Is More Than Staying Consistent

Imagine a scenario where a golfer makes a poor shot. An undisciplined player might react in frustration, allowing the disappointment to influence subsequent shots, which, in turn, leads to a downward spiral of poor performance. A disciplined player, on the other hand, sees this as an opportunity for learning and growth. They take a moment to analyze what went wrong and how they can improve. This approach, built on discipline, transforms an error into a learning experience, building mental resilience over time.

Golf also teaches discipline through the process of setting and achieving goals. These goals can range from mastering a particular skill to achieving a certain score in a tournament. When a player sets a goal, they are essentially making a commitment to themselves. The discipline to keep this commitment, to persist despite challenges, is a crucial aspect of personal growth and development. In this sense, the golf course becomes a classroom for character development, imparting life lessons that go beyond the boundaries of the sport.

Discipline is also essential in maintaining focus and resisting distractions. During a tournament, golfers must remain focused on their game, regardless of how their competitors are faring. The discipline required to keep their minds from wandering or succumbing to anxiety is a testament to their mental control, making each tournament not just a competition with other players but also a personal test of their discipline and mental toughness. Discipline in golf goes beyond the physicality of practice. It forms the bedrock of mental toughness and personal development, turning the sport into a life-long journey of learning and growth. For our young golfers and their parents, embracing this aspect of the game might just be the most rewarding part of the golfing journey.

Why Is Discipline So Hard?

Discipline can be a tough task to master, not just in golf but in any aspect of life. The core of the challenge is twofold: knowing what to do and consistently doing it, even when faced with adversity. Both are formidable challenges.

Think of discipline like steering a boat in a stormy sea. The course is plotted, the destination clear, but amidst the roaring waves and gusty winds, maintaining the right course is incredibly hard. It requires constant attention, relentless adjustment, and the will to resist veering off the path, despite the strain. Much like this analogy, golfers, especially young ones, are often like excited sailors venturing out to sea, their minds filled with dreams of discovery and adventure but lacking a solid strategy or a reliable compass. They embark on their journey relying on their talent and enthusiasm but without a strategic plan. And therein lies the problem. Just like the gambler going against the house, the odds are inherently stacked against golfers who play without a strategy. They may enjoy sporadic victories, but in the long run, their lack of strategy will lead to more losses than wins, much like a gambler relying on luck against the mathematically calculated odds of the casino.

Many young golfers are never explicitly taught to play strategically. Instead, they are encouraged to focus on perfecting their swing or hitting impressive shots, while the critical aspect of strategizing and making small, consistent decisions is overlooked. It's like teaching a new sailor how to hoist the sail without teaching them how to read a map or navigate the waters. Small, consistent decisions in golf—like choosing the right club for a particular shot, deciding when to play it safe, and when to take risks—are the fundamental building blocks to achieving big goals. It's like a ship's captain making small adjustments to the vessel's direction, each insignificant on its own but collectively leading the ship safely to the desired destination despite the tempest.

Golf is not a realm of extravagant gambles; rather, it revolves around calculated risks and strategic deliberation. Just as a casino doesn't rely on a single game to secure its winnings, golfers shouldn't depend on a single impressive shot to win their game. Instead, it's the accumulation of carefully planned, small decisions that guide a golfer to victory, just as the casino accumulates small, steady profits over a series of games, steadily piling up the chips. If young golfers learn this philosophy early on, they will play not as gamblers hoping for a lucky strike but as thoughtful strategists, systematically working toward their goals. It's not the flashy, impulsive gamble that wins the game but the calm, calculated strategy that eventually beats the odds.

Discipline in golf is about consistency, resilience, and strategic thinking. It's about being the steadfast captain of the ship, not the excited gambler betting against the house. It's about seeing beyond the immediate shot and understanding the long game. It's about the willingness to take calculated risks and the resilience to stick with the strategy, even when the tide seems to be against you. Above all, it's about understanding that big goals are achieved not through flashy tricks but through a series of small, consistent, strategic decisions.

Discipline Is Tougher for Young Athletes

Younger athletes, much like their counterparts in other disciplines, often face a daunting challenge—appreciating the power of small actions and consistent behavior in reaching their goals. This concept can seem counterintuitive, especially in a world that often highlights overnight success and spectacular victories. Imagine trying to explain to a young, vibrant tree that its strength lies not in the beauty of its blossoms or the sweetness of its fruits but rather in the silent growth of its roots, expanding ever so slowly beneath the surface. This is analogous to teaching young golfers the importance of small actions, consistency, and discipline in their pursuit of excellence.

It's natural for young golfers to be drawn toward the spectacular, the impressive shots, and the trophy-winning moments. However, true mastery in golf, as in life, is often the result of doing the same thing over and over again, refining minute details, and making small adjustments. What we need to communicate to our young golfers is that every small decision they make on the golf course, from club selection, stance, swing, and shot trajectory, is akin to a brick in the foundation of a mighty fortress. These bricks may seem mundane, even tedious, individually. But stacked together, over time, they form the very foundation of greatness.

Experiencing success, of course, plays a crucial role in boosting self-confidence and reinforcing positive behavior. A single victory can ignite a spark that can turn into an unquenchable flame. However, while these victories are important, they are often the product of countless hours spent on perfecting the basics, making the right decisions, and adhering to a solid strategy. But success, like a fair-weather friend, is often fleeting. In golf, as in life, there are wins, and there are losses. This is where mental toughness comes into play. Building mental toughness is like constructing a lighthouse that stands unflinching amidst the tempest, guiding the ship safely toward its destination.

Mental toughness allows young golfers to weather the storm of defeats, setbacks, and disappointments. It helps them understand that these setbacks are not a reflection of their potential but are merely stepping stones toward greater success. It is mental toughness that helps them stick to their strategy, persist in their practice, and believe in the process, even when immediate results are not forthcoming.

Teaching discipline to young golfers is akin to equipping them with the necessary navigational tools to voyage through the tumultuous seas of golfing challenges. It's about nurturing their understanding that the road to greatness is paved with small, consistent actions and decisions bolstered by mental resilience and an unwavering commitment to the game. It's about helping them see that in the grand scheme of their golfing journey, they should strive not to be the gambler living for the moment, but the steady, resilient casino, playing for the long haul.

The Key to Developing Discipline

Golf transcends being solely a test of physical prowess; it stands as an arena where mental discipline reigns supreme. A good golf swing is a blend of the right mechanics and the right mindset. If you've ever wondered what separates an average player from a great one, it's often their disciplined approach to the game.

Studying Your Thoughts and Emotions

The foundation of self-discipline in golf is being mindful of your thoughts and emotions. Just as you would study the landscape of a course, you need to examine the terrain of your mind. This doesn't mean constantly over-analyzing your thoughts but rather practicing mindfulness—being present and aware without judgment.

Think of it like taking a picture. Your focus determines what you capture—your main subject. But discipline keeps the frame steady. Without discipline, your focus may shift, blur, or lose the subject entirely. Therefore, discipline helps you direct your focus effectively.

Building Mental Discipline in Golf: A Strategy Guide

1. Control Fear: Fear is often born from past experiences. Choose not to let your past dictate your present game. Visualize a successful shot, and feel the emotion of triumph to dispel any lingering fear.

2. Uphold Integrity: Adhering to the rules of golf and a code of conduct promotes self-esteem and minimizes distractions. Honesty about your performance fosters a respectful and focused mindset.

3. Employ Course Management: Adopt a conservative approach when you're not playing your best. Increase your chances of a lower score by strategically positioning your shots.

4. Maintain Present-Moment Focus: Leave your ego at home. Replace self-doubting thoughts with affirmations like "I can..." or "I am..."

5. Play the Odds: Make sure to choose shots that you're confident in to avoid getting into difficult situations.

6. Be Decisive: After analyzing all the factors that influence your shot choice, trust your decision. Doubt can only undermine your performance.

Discipline in Action: Tiger Woods's Example

Tiger Woods, a name synonymous with golfing greatness, demonstrates the power of disciplined thinking. Despite numerous potential negative distractions, including past injuries, personal issues, and intense pressure, Woods won the 2019 Masters, demonstrating incredible mental discipline.

Woods kept his attention focused on what he could control: his game. His strategy was to be patient, manage his thoughts, and maintain his focus. Even when many possible distractions arose, he kept his mind disciplined and focused on the task at hand.

Similar to Woods, one can focus their attention on thoughts that enhance their performance while effectively managing any possible distractions. A conscious conversation with yourself about your strategy and goals for each shot can help maintain your mental discipline and steer you toward success.

Developing discipline in golf is about directing your focus, controlling your emotions, and staying mindful. By mastering these elements, you will enhance your performance and enjoyment of the beautiful and challenging game of golf. Parents and teens alike can learn from the mental strategies in golf, applying them not just on the course but in every area of life where focus, discipline, and resilience are key.

Turning Consistency into Habits

Habits are formed when we repetitively do the same thing consistently. Whether it's brushing your teeth before bed, lacing up your sneakers for an early morning run, or practicing your golf swing, the more you perform a certain action, the more it engrains into your routine and becomes second nature.

Discipline Plays a Key Role in Building Routines

Discipline is your internal compass, helping you navigate through the myriad distractions life throws your way. It's the practice of training oneself to adhere to a certain code of behavior, despite the surrounding circumstances. A powerful tool, discipline fuels the drive to be consistent, which, in turn, helps in establishing habits. It's the bridge that connects the goals and their accomplishment.

Discipline Reinforces Actions That Make up Routines

Routines are established through repetition. Once an action becomes a routine, it's like a well-trodden path in your mind. However, sticking to a routine isn't always easy. It's here that discipline steps in. It reinforces the action, giving it strength and resilience. Discipline helps you stick to your routine when the initial enthusiasm has worn off and the reality of hard work sets in.

Routines Help Replace Bad Habits With Better Ones

The beauty of a routine is that it can be adjusted to phase out bad habits and introduce better ones. If you are disciplined enough, you can rewire your routine to incorporate healthier habits. The key is to replace a bad habit with a good one and make that good habit part of your daily routine.

Identifying Routines for Your Play Style

Understanding your play style and integrating it into your routine is vital to improving your game. This applies whether you're practicing sports or any other skill. For instance, in golf, the routine can be broken down into three parts:

1. The warm-up routine: This involves the preparation phase, where you ready your body and mind for the game.

2. Before the shot/the setup: This phase is where you focus, plan your shot, and execute your strategy.

3. After the shot: This is where you analyze your shot, learn from any mistakes, and plan your next move accordingly.

Develop Routines to Improve Your Game

Developing routines that enhance your performance is crucial in leveling up your game. This development is threefold:

1. Analyzing your game: Scrutinize your performance. Understand your strengths and weaknesses. Learning from each game will help you evolve and improve.

2. Finding areas of improvement: Be honest and identify the aspects you need to work on. These areas become your focus for practice and improvement.

3. Practice Plan: Structure your practice sessions strategically. Dedicate a specific amount of time to improve each weakness and sharpen each strength.

Areas beyond technical skills also matter. For instance, physical fitness, mental toughness, and strategic thinking play a significant role in overall performance. Your routine should holistically incorporate all these aspects for maximum improvement.

Stories to Inspire: John Rahm—Keeping Calm With Discipline

Every once in a while, the world of sports brings us a tale of incredible transformation and success. Jon Rahm's journey toward victory at the U.S. Open Golf Championship is one such story that serves as a testament to the power of self-discipline and emotional self-control. Jon Rahm, a supremely talented golfer, was notorious for his volcanic temperament. His impatience and frustration often tainted his performance, masking his sheer skill and potential. However, the arrival of his son, Kepa, marked a turning point in Jon's life and career.

Being a father, Rahm realized, meant being a role model. He was no longer just a golfer on a course but also a figure his son would look up to, and he decided to shed the tantrums that once cast a shadow over his accomplishments. It was a shift toward emotional self-control and discipline, a significant transformation that proved to be a game-changer.

Rahm's transformation became evident during the U.S. Open. In the midst of intense competition, Jon Rahm, poised and calm, drained a pair of birdie putts that seemed nothing short of miraculous. A 25-foot birdie putt on No. 17 followed by a 17-footer for birdie on 18 are moments that will forever be engraved in the annals of golf history. What was his secret? Jon Rahm had harnessed the power of discipline and emotional self-control, the two ingredients that had been missing from his game. This newfound tranquility did not dilute his grit; rather, it amplified it, lending him a resilience that was previously absent. Each miss seemed to affect him less; every mistake became a lesson rather than a failure.

When Rahm missed a birdie putt on hole 14, he didn't explode in frustration or self-blame. Instead, he uttered four words that spoke volumes of his transformation, "That was a good putt." Rahm was not only in control of his golf swing but also of his emotions. This equilibrium paved the way for his victory at the U.S. Open.

Rahm's transformation and success are an embodiment of the axiom that discipline and patience indeed bear sweet fruit. His journey serves as a beacon of inspiration not only for aspiring golfers but also for anyone grappling with the challenge of mastering self-control and discipline. So, parents and teens alike, remember the story of Jon Rahm. The road to your goals might be paved with frustrating obstacles and disappointments. Still, with discipline and emotional self-control, not only can these challenges be tackled, but they can also become stepping stones to grand success, just like they did for Jon Rahm, the U.S. Open Champion.

Teeing Up: Actionable Steps to Cultivate Discipline

This chapter has examined the integral role of discipline and time management in enhancing mental toughness in golf. Now let's boil down these insights into actionable steps that can help refine discipline in both coaches and athletes.

For the Coach

1. Instill the Importance of Discipline: Explain the significance of discipline in golf to your athletes, emphasizing its role in improving mental toughness, consistency, and strategic play.

2. Foster Strategic Thinking: Encourage your athletes to think strategically, illustrating how small, consistent decisions lead to the achievement of big goals.

3. Promote Mindfulness: Teach your athletes the practice of mindfulness. Help them understand how studying their thoughts and emotions can enhance their focus and discipline on the course.

4. Help Establish Routines: Assist your athletes in identifying and developing effective routines. This could be pre-shot routines, post-shot routines, or warm-up routines. Routines help instill discipline and replace unhelpful habits with better ones.

5. Facilitate Regular Analysis: Encourage your athletes to consistently analyze their performance to identify areas for improvement, thus fostering a disciplined approach to improvement.

For the Athlete

1. Understand Discipline: Grasp the concept of discipline and its role in enhancing your golf performance. Recognize that consistent practice and a structured approach to learning can contribute significantly to mental toughness.

2. Think Strategically: Cultivate strategic thinking. Learn to appreciate how small, consistent actions can lead to significant improvements in your game over time.

3. Practice Mindfulness: Engage in mindfulness practices to better understand your thoughts and emotions. This can help you focus better on the course and improve your discipline.

4. Develop Routines: Establish routines that suit your play

style. This can help reinforce discipline and replace unproductive habits with beneficial ones.

5. Analyze Regularly: Make it a habit to analyze your performance regularly. Identify areas for improvement and develop a disciplined practice plan to work on these areas.

Remember, discipline is a product of consistent effort and practice. Incorporating these steps into your golfing routine will gradually build your mental toughness, leading to enhanced performance on the course.

Conclusion

It is pivotal to emphasize the critical role of discipline in golf. As underlined through the lens of Tiger Woods's perspective and Jon Rahm's transformation, discipline serves as a cornerstone of improvement and mental toughness. The practice of discipline helps engrave consistency into a routine, thereby molding a golfer's raw potential into refined skill. The process might be challenging, especially for the younger golfers who are yet to realize the value of strategic play and small, consistent decisions. Nevertheless, mastering discipline is truly transformative. It is more than just a tool for learning effectively; it's a catalyst for mindfulness, a director for focus, and a controller of emotions. Through disciplined practice and mindful repetition, every golfer can unlock the beauty of their tomorrow, continually becoming a better version of their today.

Chapter 5: Skill #4–Unshakeable Self-Belief

"Confidence is the 15th and most important club in the bag," Lydia Ko, the young golf prodigy, famously declared. This simple statement captures the essence of a truth that rings true not only in the world of golf but also in the larger scheme of life.

Lydia's journey, if viewed as a landscape, is littered with the markers of her unwavering self-belief. She embarked on her professional career at an age when most of her peers were focused on high school dramas. Through the pressure, the expectations, the applause, and the criticisms, her self-belief has been her lighthouse in the tumultuous sea of professional golf, steadfast and bright, guiding her ship through storms and fog toward victory and acclaim.

In golf, as in life, confidence and self-belief play a pivotal role. The game of golf is as much about conquering the mind as it is about skillful shots. When you stand on the green with the club in your hand and the hole far in the distance, it's not just the wind or the swing that you have to worry about. It's that voice in your head, questioning if you can make the shot, doubting your skill and ability. That voice can cloud your mind, fill your body with anxiety, and affect the very control over your movements that are crucial for a good swing.

Proactive versus reactive confidence becomes a deciding factor in this scenario. Proactive confidence is where you dictate the narrative, controlling your self-belief, whereas reactive confidence allows the circumstances and external factors to control your belief in yourself.

When self-doubt strikes, it's essential to regain control, to shift focus from the negative to the positive. It's vital to step back and objectively evaluate not just the current round but also the bigger picture of your game. You must question the veracity of your negative thoughts, identify the root cause of your self-doubt, and try to redirect this energy into something productive.

Building confidence and self-belief isn't a one-day task. It's akin to constructing a skyscraper, with preparation as its foundation. This preparation encompasses every aspect, from perfecting your equipment to honing your technical skills, developing a strategic mindset, maintaining physical fitness, and fortifying your mental resilience. Remember, consistency and discipline are the mortar and bricks of this skyscraper of confidence.

The inspiring story of Jason Day's victory at the 2018 Wells Fargo tournament serves as a testament to this. After wrestling with self-doubt and overcoming it with his unwavering self-belief, he emerged victorious, proving to us that confidence, indeed, is the most important club in the bag. His victory is a shining example of the power of unshakeable self-belief.

By the end of this chapter, you'll understand that self-belief isn't an innate quality but a skill that can be honed and perfected. You'll also learn to navigate your way through self-doubt, understand the significance of preparation, and develop unshakeable confidence in your game, taking you one step closer to becoming an exceptional golfer.

A Game of Confidence

In analyzing the profound impact of confidence and self-doubt on one's performance in golf, it's crucial to perceive the game not just as a physical challenge but equally as a mental one. It is aptly described as a Game of Confidence. Essentially, the golf course is a stage upon which players put on a display of both physical skill and mental fortitude. Confidence in golf, akin to any sport, can be the defining factor that separates the great from the average. To consistently perform well, a player must harbor an unwavering belief in their abilities. This confidence acts as a mental shield, bolstering resilience in the face of adversity and enabling the player to maintain focus despite setbacks. For instance, a confident golfer perceives a missed shot not as a failure but as an opportunity for learning and improvement.

Self-Doubt and Performance

Self-doubt, an inherent part of the human psyche, can emerge as a significant impediment to performance. It can surface at any point—before a swing or in the aftermath of a poor shot—and has the potential to undermine a golfer's performance. At the heart of self-doubt is a fear of failure that can give rise to stress and anxiety, triggering the fight-or-flight response, a physiological reaction designed for survival.

Though this response served our ancestors well when confronted by a physical threat, it hampers the execution of delicate motor skills required in sports like golf. The physiological changes associated with this response, such as dilated pupils and an increase in adrenaline, can make it challenging to maintain visual and mental focus, leading to heightened difficulty in controlling movements. Self-doubt and the ensuing stress can cause involuntary muscle tension, making fine motor control virtually impossible.

Subconscious Mind Taking Over

An important manifestation of this stress is the subconscious mind assuming control, a carryover from our primal instincts. When this happens, the mind attempts to respond to perceived threats (in this case, self-doubt) in the same way it would to physical danger. This reaction narrows the passageway between our conscious and subconscious minds, switching off attentional and emotional control centers deemed unnecessary for survival. Therefore, developing strategies to manage self-doubt and nurture confidence is paramount. By implementing scientifically proven techniques, golfers can learn to focus their attention, relax their bodies, and calm their nerves. This approach allows access to the memory centers responsible for the automatic reproduction of one's best swing or stroke.

Confidence isn't just about playing well but also about feeling good overall about your game; confidence in golf extends beyond the execution of good strokes. It's also about having faith in your abilities, trusting in your decisions, and having overall positive feelings about your game. Confidence acts as a golfer's mental armor, protecting and enabling them to perform optimally even in high-pressure situations. It also affects how a player reacts to both good and bad performances.

Proactive vs. Reactive Confidence

The key distinction between proactive and reactive confidence lies in who holds the reins: do you control your confidence, or does your confidence control you?

Proactive Confidence

This is the choice to sustain belief in one's abilities regardless of temporary setbacks. Great athletes like Jordan Spieth showcase proactive confidence. They base their confidence on the positive experiences they've had in the game and the work they've invested in it. This kind of confidence is built on a strong foundation, so minor hiccups in performance don't easily shake it.

Reactive Confidence

On the other hand, some players allow small setbacks or external influences to damage their self-belief. This is known as reactive confidence. Here, a player lets minor failures or challenges determine their confidence level. They may let negative comments or poor performance significantly impact their self-assurance, often to their detriment.

Cultivating confidence is a continuous process. Key methods include comprehensive preparation; understanding one's strengths, limitations, and triggers; getting good coaching; setting clear goals; developing a positive internal voice; focusing on successful actions rather than mistakes; and paying attention to the development process, not just the outcome. Remember, confidence isn't just a factor in your golf game—it's a skill that translates to all aspects of life, from business and career to relationships and any other performance-based activity. The process of building and maintaining confidence provides an invaluable skill set that is applicable across various life scenarios. It's an investment in yourself that pays dividends in all areas of life.

What to Do When Self-Doubt Strikes

Overcoming self-doubt is a universal struggle, especially in a sport like golf, where the mind plays an equally, if not more, significant role as physical strength. When the cloud of self-doubt strikes, it's crucial to navigate through it efficiently and effectively. Here's a roadmap.

Avoid the All or Nothing Mindset

Whether you're a golfer or not, it's common to evaluate performance in binary terms. You either win, or you lose; you're either perfect or a failure. This "all or nothing" mindset ignores the nuances and complexities of performance evaluation, not considering the positives even in the losses. As the adage goes, failure is the stepping stone to success.

Teen golfers need to understand that losing doesn't necessarily mean they played poorly. Dissecting every mistake and berating oneself is counterproductive. Instead, recognizing the positives in one's game, irrespective of winning or losing, contributes to confidence. Losing may hurt, but it also serves as a potent motivation to improve.

Remember Justin Thomas at the 2020 Masters. Despite finishing fourth, he still found positives about his performance, which kept his confidence intact and motivated him to work on his game. He realized that not every shot was perfect, but that every shot was a learning experience.

So, every time you play, avoid the "all or nothing" mindset. Think of your performance on a scale from 1-10. Remember, not every day will be an "A-game" day, but there's always something to learn and improve.

Taming Self-Doubt in Golf

In the heat of the game, when doubt rears its ugly head, it's essential to view it as a signal to heighten your focus rather than an impediment.

Self-doubt can actually push you into The Zone, a mental state where you are fully immersed in and enjoy the activity, playing better golf. When you encounter that intimidating tee shot in the future, keep in mind the principle derived from Newton's Law. Remember that every action produces a corresponding and opposite reaction. For every self-doubt, there's an opportunity for self-belief. Flip the narrative and turn negative thoughts into positive mantras.

When a negative doubt arises, reframe it as a positive sign to reorganize your thoughts toward a positive outcome. For instance, if you worry about chunking the next shot, think about how you have been striking the ball perfectly all day, and it wouldn't surprise you if you hit this shot next to the hole.

Your thoughts are powerful tools, and you can use them to channel your nervous energy into something productive. Develop a positive mantra for yourself, like "I CHOOSE TO FEEL NOW." This mantra signifies that you are in control, you remember the feel of a perfect shot, you are focused on your target, and you're ready to take action now. Understanding and reinterpreting doubts and nervous feelings as signals to heighten your focus can bring a deep, zone-like calming focus. This reframing can transform nervous energies into positive adrenaline, propelling you toward your best performance.

Take a Step Back

Evaluating your performance objectively is crucial. Often, it's easier to lose sight of the forest for the trees. You might end up focusing excessively on a single shot or round, ignoring your overall progress.

Reflect on your performance over time, not just on the immediate outcome. Identify patterns and areas of improvement. Where is the self-doubt coming from? Is it a specific aspect of your game or general performance anxiety? Answering these questions can help you focus on the right areas and overcome self-doubt.

Choose How You Feel

Your response to self-doubt and negative thoughts can make a significant difference. Accepting that these feelings are natural and are even beneficial can change your approach to dealing with them. Instead of worrying about them, channel these feelings into something productive.

Think about your target, focusing on where you want the shot to go. Be in the moment, feel the club in your hands, the turf beneath your shoes, the wind in your face. Channel all this awareness into hitting the perfect shot. In a nutshell, golf is a mental game. Dealing with self-doubt is about understanding and reframing your thoughts, focusing on the positives, and choosing how to respond to negative feelings. Remember, every shot, every round, every game is a learning experience. Embrace them all, and you'll find your confidence soaring, one swing at a time.

How to Build Confidence and Self-Belief

A captivating journey awaits every young golfer on the fairway, a journey that ultimately leads to the treasure chest of self-confidence and belief. Jack Nicklaus, a golf legend, once remarked, "Confidence is believing in your own ability, knowing what you have to do to win. My confidence was developed through preparation." In a nutshell, the seed of confidence germinates from the soil of preparation.

The world of golf is a complex interplay of physical prowess, technical precision, strategic thinking, and psychological strength. Of these aspects, however, the most influential is perhaps the last one: the power of the mind. It's crucial to emphasize the impact of your mental state on your game, as the difference between an impressive swing at the practice range and a faltered swing during the game is often merely a matter of mindset.

So, what are the stepping stones to nurturing this self-belief, and how do we lay them down through preparation? Let's take a swing at them.

Equipment Needs

Are you equipped for success? Ensuring that you have the right gear, from clubs suited to your unique swing and height to weather-appropriate attire, is a vital part of preparation. A golf bag should be a treasure trove of essentials: balls, tees, rangefinder, towel, extra glove, and even first aid essentials like band-aids and sunscreen. Your equipment is your silent ally on the field, ready to boost your confidence through every hole.

Technical Skills

There's no substitute for knowing your swing, understanding the impact of the ball's lie, reading the greens, and setting up correctly. A reliable and consistent pre-shot routine gives your game stability, making you feel in control. This mastery over the technical aspects empowers you with the confidence to face any challenge on the course.

Strategic Approach

Victory in golf isn't just about getting the ball in the hole; it's about doing so with the fewest strokes possible. Thus, preparation requires formulating a robust plan for each course you play. Consider the course conditions, the weather, and the hole layouts. The more adept you are at this strategic side of golf, the more confident you'll feel as you step onto the green.

Physical Preparedness

Are you fit for the game? Do you have a pre-round warm-up routine? Good nutrition and hydration are also parts of this preparation. Knowing your physical abilities and limitations and preparing accordingly, can make a significant difference in your confidence level and performance.

Mindset and Visualization

The most crucial element of all is your mindset. Having a positive attitude, being ready to handle a spectrum of emotions on the course, and pre-visualizing your shots are integral parts of mental preparation. Remember, confidence, as defined by Albert Bandura, the father of self-efficacy theory, is "the belief in one's ability to succeed in specific situations or accomplish a task." This belief can be fortified by visualizing successful outcomes.

Cultivate Patience

Patience is indeed a virtue, and this is especially true in golf. Golf requires a lot of patience and the ability to maintain composure even when things are not going your way. Learning to handle frustration effectively can lead to an increase in confidence over time. Remind yourself that golf is a game that takes time to master. Don't rush the process; instead, appreciate each step of your journey.

Establish Routines

Routines help to create a sense of consistency and predictability, which can lead to increased confidence. These can be pre-shot routines or a particular practice routine. Familiar patterns can create a comfort zone that can boost your self-belief. Embrace the routine, knowing that each step is leading you toward becoming a more confident golfer.

Embrace Your Unique Playing Style

Just as each golfer has their unique swing, each golfer also has their own unique style of play. Embrace your unique playing style, and don't feel pressured to change it to fit the mold. This not only makes the game more enjoyable but also helps build your confidence as you recognize and appreciate your unique abilities.

Keep Learning and Improving

No matter how skilled you are, there is always room for improvement. Keep an open mind and be willing to learn new techniques or strategies. This can improve your game and increase your confidence as you see yourself growing and becoming better. Remember, every champion was once a learner.

The Need for Mental Fortitude in Golf

When on the fairway, every golfer, whether seasoned or a novice, faces a variety of challenges. These can include everything from first-tee jitters to overthinking about swing mechanics. Often, golfers tend to lose themselves in the technical details, forgetting the essence of the game: to have fun, be creative, and enjoy the moment. This tendency not only creates unnecessary tension but also undermines their performance.

Meditation: A Tool for Mental Strength

Meditation can be a powerful tool to overcome these hurdles. However, it is essential to understand that meditation is not just about relaxation. Instead, it cultivates mental strength and resilience.

Meditation practices enable golfers to center their minds, boosting their ability to remain calm, relaxed, and focused. These elements, in turn, significantly influence their performance on the course.

Activating Confidence Through Meditation

It's a common misconception that confidence only stems from performing well. In reality, self-confidence is built through a belief in one's abilities and the conviction that they can improve. Here, meditation plays a crucial role.

By visualizing successful shots and positive outcomes, players can reinforce self-belief, thus activating confidence. Regular meditation practice helps to embed these images in the mind, making them a potent source of self-assurance.

Cultivating Control With Meditation

Another invaluable aspect of meditation is its ability to nurture control. On the golf course, being in control of your thoughts and emotions is critical to staying in the zone. Like the practice of deep breathing, meditating aids in developing this control. It encourages golfers to let go of conscious judgment and maintain their focus on the game at hand.

Responding Positively to Mistakes

A common setback for golfers is the inability to bounce back from mistakes. This issue often arises from a lack of mental resilience. Regular meditation can help players respond positively to their mistakes, accept them, and move on with a concentrated effort on the next shot. Meditation helps to foster a "present-moment" mindset, freeing players from the shackles of past errors and future anxieties. In essence, it facilitates a constructive recovery from any setback, leading to a more resilient mental approach to the game.

Embracing meditation can remarkably enhance a golfer's mental prowess, thereby refining their performance on the course. It helps build mental strength, activate confidence, and cultivate control—key components for any successful golfer. So, whether you are a teen embarking on your golfing journey or a parent seeking to elevate your teen's game, consider incorporating meditation into your training regime for a holistic approach to golf.

The journey of preparation isn't just about stepping onto the course with the right clubs. It's also about stepping onto the green with the right mindset. Thus, confidence isn't a gift you're born with; it's an attribute you develop through relentless preparation. Your willingness to embrace this thorough preparation not only gives you a realistic understanding of effective golf but also injects you with the confidence to play the best game of your life.

Stories to Inspire: Saving the Day

In the high-pressure world of professional golf, the toughest opponent is often not the challenging course nor the skilled competitors, but rather, one's own mind. This was the case for Jason Day during the 2018 Wells Fargo tournament—a testament to the universal struggle of self-doubt.

Jason Day, a talented golfer known for his ability to focus and execute shots with precision, found himself wrestling with doubt and insecurity on the final day of the tournament. In a surprising twist, he missed more than half the fairways, hit a disastrous shot into the water on the 14th hole, and seemed to lose his way, squandering a three-shot lead. However, it was his response to these setbacks that revealed his true character. Amidst the mounting pressure and the rising tide of self-doubt, Day chose to confront his inner demons head-on. "I was kind of battling demons there inside my head," he confessed. And yet, Day pushed forward, reminding himself that "you somehow have just to get rid of those thoughts and just push forward."

Rather than surrendering to his insecurities, Day resolved to concentrate on his short game, which was working well for him. It was a wise strategy. Despite his struggles on the green, he found redemption and strength in his short game. It saved his day and, arguably, his tournament.

His focus paid off. Displaying remarkable resilience and mental fortitude, Day managed to birdie two of his final three holes, ultimately securing the Wells Fargo Championship.

This story acts as a poignant illustration of the significance of maintaining a positive mindset. Despite encountering challenges and self-doubt, Day was able to transform his performance, not by altering his external circumstances, but by shifting his perspective.

Like Day, we all face moments of doubt and uncertainty. In these moments, it's essential to remember that the key to overcoming these trials often lies in our minds. By focusing on what's going right rather than dwelling on what's going wrong, we can bolster our confidence and resilience. Day's story is proof that the battle of the mind is indeed a winnable one—with perseverance, focus, and a positive outlook. It's a lesson that holds true, whether you're navigating the challenging greens of a golf course or the trials and tribulations of everyday life.

Teeing Up: Actionable Steps to Cultivate Unshakeable Self-Belief

This chapter has dissected the powerful role of self-belief and confidence in golf. We have discovered how they can impact performance and ways to foster them. Here, we break down these lessons into actionable steps you can apply as a coach or an athlete.

For the Coach

1. Explain the Role of Confidence: Illustrate to your athletes how confidence and self-belief can dramatically affect their performance. Ensure they understand the implications of self-doubt and its potential to induce stress and anxiety.

2. Teach Emotional Control: Help your athletes gain emotional control, teaching them to handle self-doubt by taking a step back and evaluating their performance objectively.

3. Foster Positive Mantras: Encourage your athletes to develop personal positive mantras that they can use to shift focus from self-doubt to self-belief.

4. Instill Trust: Cultivate trust in your athletes by constantly reassuring them of their abilities. A lack of trust often gives birth to self-doubt.

5. Promote Consistent Practice: Underscore the importance of regular and disciplined practice. Consistency not only refines technical skills but also prepares the mind for challenges, boosting confidence.

For the Athlete

1. Understand Confidence: Embrace the concept of confidence and its impact on your golf performance. Recognize the detrimental effects of self-doubt and work toward eliminating it.

2. Develop Emotional Control: Learn to manage your emotions, especially when self-doubt strikes. Analyze your performance objectively and focus on overall progress rather than isolated instances.

3. Create a Positive Mantra: Establish a personal positive mantra that you can use to shift focus from negativity and self-doubt. This mantra can be a source of motivation and a tool to regain focus.

4. Trust Yourself: Cultivate trust in your abilities. Understand that trust is a manifestation of self-belief and that doubting your abilities can inhibit your performance.

5. Engage in Regular Practice: Incorporate consistent practice into your routine. Regular practice is key to refining your skills, preparing your mind for challenges, and, ultimately, boosting your confidence.

Remember, confidence and self-belief are not innate traits but skills that can be developed. The above steps can aid in fostering an unshakeable belief in yourself, enabling you to thrive even under pressure. Embrace the journey of self-belief, and enjoy the transformation it brings to your golf game.

Conclusion

Confidence is a key player in the game of golf, acting as an invisible but impactful club in a golfer's bag. This chapter highlighted that a proactive approach to confidence can combat self-doubt, reducing its negative effects on performance.

We provided strategies for tackling self-doubt and fostering self-belief, emphasizing the importance of emotional control, objective performance evaluation, and positivity. Preparation, practice, trust in oneself, and reframing negative thoughts were also identified as crucial in building confidence. Lastly, Jason Day's triumph in the 2018 Wells Fargo tournament underscored the power of an unshakeable self-belief in overcoming adversity. Ultimately, confidence and self-belief, when cultivated diligently, can lead to significant victories on and off the golf course.

Chapter 6: Skill #5—Setting the Right Goals

Golf champion Rory McIlroy once confessed, "I used to write down that I want to win five times, I want to win a major, I want to win The Race to Dubai, I want to win the FedEx Cup... but I can't control it. There are so many other variables in there. I'd rather set goals that are objective and measurable, that I'm in control of."

Picture the serene landscape of a golf course. Now, imagine McIlroy studying the terrain, calculating the force and trajectory required for his next stroke. His goal isn't just about winning a tournament, but it's the culmination of a series of smaller, attainable, and measurable objectives. Every stroke, every swing, each a precise target set with a broader vision in mind.

When it comes to golf, just like in our everyday lives, the significance of establishing appropriate objectives cannot be emphasized enough.

It's not just about setting targets but rather about aligning these targets with your personal aspirations, capabilities, and the reality of your environment. Think of goals as the guiding stars, not the distant, twinkling lights in the night sky, but those navigational tools that ancient seafarers used to sail vast, uncharted oceans. They are objective yet personal. Tangible, yet intrinsically tied to our emotional and mental well-being. Achievable, yet constantly pushing us beyond our comfort zones.

McIlroy's wisdom extends beyond the greens. Goals, he insists, must be rooted in reality. Not having goals that you genuinely want or setting unachievable ones can lead to failure and frustration, undermining your confidence and robbing you of your motivation. So, how do we set the right goals? As we delve into this chapter, we'll examine the SMART framework—a formula that ensures that your goals are Specific, Measurable, Attainable, Realistic, and Time-sensitive. Furthermore, we'll explore how to balance short-term achievements with long-term aspirations and the significance of holding yourself accountable. From the fairways, we'll draw inspiration from another golf champion: Justin Thomas. A tale that underscores the transformational power of personal, motivating goals. But remember, in setting your sights, it's not about mirroring someone else's path but about creating one that is uniquely yours.

In the words of McIlroy, "I can't control winning a tournament... I'd rather set goals that are objective and measurable, that I'm in control of." As we navigate this chapter, let's learn to set the right goals, not just those in our control but also those that empower us to strive for greatness in every swing of life.

Goals and Golf

As affirmed by experienced golfers, golf extends beyond a mere game; it embodies a disciplined pursuit. Just as the path of a golf ball is driven by force, direction, and intention, so too is the progression of our lives. This chapter delves into the power of goal setting in golf and explores how this game of skill and precision mirrors the journey of life itself.

Goals, Golf, and You: A Symbiotic Relationship

Imagine stepping onto the golf course, a club in hand, with no target to aim for. Chances are, you'd be standing there, clueless and purposeless. That's precisely the role of goals in our lives and especially in golf. Goals lend direction, shape our paths, and dictate our actions. Just as golf players direct their swing toward the hole, we direct our efforts toward achieving our goals.

Targets in golf are synonymous with goals in life. You can't hit a hole-in-one without a hole to aim for, and you can't progress without clear, defined goals. Setting goals and targets is about directing your attention on a broader scale, focusing not only on the task at hand but also on the bigger picture.

The Diverse Landscape of Goals

Goals in golf, much like those in life, come in different shapes and sizes. Let's explore these varying goals, each as important as the next:

- Technical Goals: These are akin to refining your golf swing or mastering a new stroke. In life, this could mean learning a new skill or honing an existing one.

- Target Goals: In golf, this might be aiming for a specific score in your next tournament. In your personal or professional life, it might look like aiming for a promotion or maintaining a specific grade point average.

- Future Goals: These are long-term goals like aspiring to win a national championship or desiring to attend a prestigious university.

Prioritizing Goals: The Key to Time Management

Setting goals isn't just about creating a wish list; it's also about prioritizing these goals in terms of their importance. This practice dictates how you allocate your time, develop your routines, and establish your habits. The more significant a goal, the more time and effort it should command.

The Psychological Impact of Goal Setting

Setting the right goals can significantly affect your mental state. Unattainable goals often result in feelings of failure and inadequacy, while goals that lack personal relevance or desire can leave you feeling unmotivated. The trick lies in finding the sweet spot—setting ambitious yet achievable goals that excite you, challenge you, and ultimately drive you toward success. Remember, a hole-in-one in golf is incredible but rare; focusing on making steady progress with each swing is a more consistent and rewarding approach.

The parallels between golf and life are numerous. Both demand patience, perseverance, and precision. Both reward those who take calculated risks and those who understand the power of focus and intent. So, as you make your way across the golf course, remember: every swing, every hole, and every game is an opportunity to learn and grow. And just like golf, life isn't about achieving perfection; it's about striving for continual improvement.

Setting SMART Goals

Let's delve deeper into the subject of goal-setting and how it can revolutionize the way you approach your aspirations and desired accomplishments. Remember, this isn't exclusive to sports or golf but also applies to any aspect of life, be it your academics, your relationships, or your personal development.

In essence, SMART is an acronym that encapsulates the five key principles of effective goal-setting: Specific, Measurable, Attainable, Realistic, and Time-sensitive.

- Specific: You need to be clear about what you want to achieve. This will give you a distinct direction and prevent you from wandering aimlessly in the pursuit of vague ideas. A goal like "I want to get better at math" is not specific. Instead, make it something like, "I want to score at least 90% on my next math test."

- Measurable: It's crucial to make your goal measurable. This means that you should be able to track your progress and determine when you've accomplished your goal. For example, improving your math skills is a broad, immeasurable goal. But, aiming for a specific score on your next test allows you to measure your success or progress.

- Attainable: Your goals should be challenging, but they must still be within your reach. The objective is to inspire motivation, not discourage you. If you're currently scoring around 70% on your math tests, for instance, a goal of scoring 95% in the next month may not be attainable. Instead, you might aim for 80% to start, which is a significant but achievable improvement.

- Realistic: It's essential that the goals you set align with your abilities and resources. Unrealistic goals can lead to frustration and discouragement. A realistic goal takes into consideration your current situation and your ability to attain it.

- Time-sensitive: Deadlines stimulate action by creating a

sense of urgency. Without a timeline, you might be tempted to start your goal tomorrow... or never. By setting a deadline for your goals, such as "I will achieve an 80% score on my next math test in four weeks," you set a clear target to work toward.

So, how does this all come together in the process of goal-setting? Let's break it down into general steps for you.

1. Decide what you want to accomplish: Clearly define what you want to achieve. This could be anything from academic success, improved athletic performance, or personal development like learning a new language.

2. Establish both immediate and future objectives: Immediate objectives refer to the targets you plan to accomplish in the foreseeable future, such as within the upcoming weeks or months. Conversely, future objectives may require several years to attain. For instance, an immediate objective could involve enhancing your academic performance for the current semester, while a future objective might entail gaining admission to a prestigious university.

3. Align your immediate objectives with your long-term aspirations: It is crucial for your immediate objectives to serve as stepping stones toward your long-term aspirations. This implies that accomplishing your immediate objectives should contribute to the realization of your long-term goals. For instance, if your long-term goal is to pursue a professional career in athletics, an immediate objective could involve joining a local sports club or improving your running speed by 10% over the next six months.

4. Write your goals down and hold yourself accountable: This gives your goals a sense of reality and substance. Also, reviewing them regularly can boost your motivation and remind you of your commitments. Share your goals with a trusted friend, family member, or mentor, and ask them to help you stay accountable.

Goal-setting is a dynamic process. Don't be afraid to revise your goals if your circumstances change. The key is to remain flexible and open-minded in your journey toward achieving your aspirations. Whether you're setting goals for yourself or helping your teen set theirs, the SMART framework is an incredibly effective tool for setting clear, achievable targets. By using this methodology, you can break down any large, seemingly unattainable goal into manageable, measurable steps.

The Right Goals for You

As a golfer (or parent of a golfer), it's essential to understand that goal-setting should be highly personalized and unique to you. What works for one person may not work for another. The "right" goals are those that align with your skills, abilities, interests, resources, and long-term aspirations. They should be challenging yet attainable, pushing you to step outside of your comfort zone but not to a point where they become frustrating or discouraging. Keep in mind that setting the right goals takes a clear understanding of your current abilities and what you genuinely want to achieve.

Process vs. Outcome

In golf, like many other activities, you can categorize goals into two main types: process goals and outcome/results goals.

Process Goals

These are about focusing on the steps or procedures necessary to perform well. They're not directly tied to the result of a game or match, but they are crucial to improving performance. For instance, a process goal could be to "Work on my short game three days a week" or "Use speed training sticks 3x per week." The beauty of process goals is that they are entirely under your control and tend to relieve the pressure because they focus on effort and learning rather than on results.

Outcome Goals

These are tied directly to the result or performance level you want to achieve. For example, an outcome goal could be "Win a tournament" or "Break 75 for the first time." While outcome goals can provide motivation, they are frequently susceptible to external factors beyond your influence, such as the performance of fellow players. Therefore, it's beneficial to balance outcome goals with process goals. Your process goals will provide a roadmap for the actions you need to take daily, which, over time, will make your outcome goals more attainable.

Practice Goals

These are specifically designed to optimize your training sessions and make the most of your practice. Examples include "Make 100 3-footers every week" or "Work on short game 2x as much as long game." Consistent, focused practice is key to improving your skills and, ultimately, your performance during matches.

On-Course Goals

On-course goals are meant to help enhance your performance during actual play. These could involve mental strategies, such as "Eliminate negative self-talk," or physical ones, like "Always go through a pre-shot routine." They are not necessarily tied to the score but are aimed at improving your in-game strategies and maintaining focus and calm on the course.

Goals Not to Aim For

While setting goals is crucial, it's equally important to avoid setting non-specific or vague goals that are hard to measure or attain. Examples include "Drive it longer," "Play more consistently," or "Hit my long irons better." Such goals lack specificity and measurability, which are key features of effective goal setting. Instead, opt for goals like "Average 275 off the tee" or "Hit 50% of greens with my 4-6 irons" that provide clear, measurable targets.

Setting goals can revolutionize your game, motivating you to continually improve your skills and aim for higher performance levels. Whether they're process, outcome, practice, or on-course goals, they provide a clear roadmap for the path you want to take. Just remember to keep them specific, measurable, attainable, realistic, and time-bound (SMART) to ensure that they are effective and truly beneficial. As you or your teen embark on this journey, remember that progress is a process, and every small step you take toward your goals is a victory in itself.

Achieving Your Goals: Embracing the Rory McIlroy Way

As a teenager, it's quite normal to get lost in the vast sea of your dreams and goals. But there's a simple way to navigate these dreams—a way popularized by the renowned professional golfer Rory McIlroy. If Rory could ride the wave of his dreams and clinch the title of Champion Golfer of the Year at the tender age of 25, what stops you? Let's explore his approach.

Rory McIlroy had a straightforward strategy to hit his targets: Process and Spot. He explains, "With my long shots, I wanted to stick to my process, the process of making a good swing, so I wasn't thinking about the end result." In a similar vein, when it came to his putting technique, Rory opted for a strategic approach by selecting a specific point on the green and focusing on rolling the ball over it, rather than solely aiming for the hole. The secret behind his success was sticking to these principles consistently, ensuring he made each small step with accuracy rather than stressing about the ultimate goal. To make your path smoother, the McIlroy Goal Setting Process can be broken down into performance goals, process goals, and spot goals.

Performance Goals

These are specific targets that Rory knew would improve his overall game over the season. For instance, he aimed to improve his stats from the previous year, like wanting his "proximity to the hole inside 150 yards to be a certain number" or "hit over 60% of fairways."

In your life, performance goals could be to get a particular grade on a test, to finish reading a book by the end of the week, or to spend a certain number of hours practicing a musical instrument.

Process Goals

Breaking down performance goals into smaller, manageable steps is where process goals come in. These are actions you have complete control over and that help in achieving your larger objectives.

To stick to Rory's example, if his performance goal was to hit over 60% of fairways, his process goals could include regular gym workouts to increase his club head speed and practicing his driving accuracy. Relating it back to your life, if your performance goal is to get an A on a test, your process goals could be to study for a certain amount of time each day, to complete practice questions, or to review and revise each chapter thoroughly.

Spot Goals

Spot goals in Rory's context refer to the specific spot he aimed at while putting, bringing his focus back to a simpler, manageable target rather than the larger, more intimidating goal. In your context, a spot goal could be completing a difficult math problem before moving on to the next chapter or learning to play a difficult section of a song on your instrument before attempting the whole piece.

Just as Rory McIlroy managed to hit those long shots and putts by simplifying his process, you can also achieve your dreams by keeping things simple. Instead of being overwhelmed by the magnitude of your goal, concentrate on taking care of the steps leading to it. Remember, life is a game where success is not measured by the final score but by the number of well-played shots. By focusing on your process and spot goals, you're setting yourself up for a great performance, regardless of the result. Just like Rory McIlroy, you can achieve your dreams by staying disciplined and focused and sticking to your process.

Stories to Inspire: How Justin Thomas Sets Goals

Justin Thomas, the renowned professional golfer, carries an intriguing habit that captures the attention of golf fans each year: he sets his goals for the season and shares them publicly only after the season ends. This approach may sound unconventional, but it illustrates how Thomas understands the power of personal goals and the motivation they inspire. Born into a family with deep roots in golf, Thomas's journey to professional success was fueled by his strong dedication, a trait he inherited from his father, Mike Thomas, a respected PGA professional. Yet, beyond this unwavering dedication, there's an essential tool that helps Thomas achieve his greatness on the green: his list of goals.

In the digital age, Thomas uses a simple yet effective way to manage his goals. He utilizes the notes app on his phone, carefully documenting his objectives before the start of each season. Whether the goals are about his swing or the number of tournaments he aims to win, Thomas keeps these ambitions to himself until the season is over. After the completion of the season, Thomas evaluates his performance against these self-set benchmarks. The sight of his goals with emojis next to them signifying whether or not they've been achieved is a testament to his commitment. Despite the occasional red "X" mark symbolizing an unfulfilled goal, he remains proud of his efforts.

Inspired by Thomas, teenagers and their parents can learn the art of goal setting by focusing on specific objectives. Short-term goals may involve refining their swing mechanics and mastering the skill of successfully executing bunker shots. The long-term goals, like Thomas's, could aim at a grander scale: winning a certain number of tournaments or achieving a specific scoring average. However, it's crucial to remember that the goal-setting process is deeply personal and subjective. While one may aspire to hit 14 greens in regulation every round, another might find satisfaction in simply enjoying the game. Both are valid, and both can fuel motivation and drive progress.

Thomas's story reminds us that it's okay not to reach all our goals. In the end, it's about the journey, the effort put in, and the personal growth that comes from pursuing these objectives. The purpose is to ignite motivation, encourage persistence, and open doors for new goals.

Thomas, the 2022 PGA Champion, stands as a beacon of how setting personal goals can lead to incredible success. But perhaps more importantly, he underscores the essence of goal setting—a tool for self-improvement and personal satisfaction, not merely a scorecard to be presented to the world. You, after all, are the one standing over the ball in the end.

Teeing Up: Actionable Steps to Set the Right Goals

Having explored the critical importance of goal-setting in golf and the value of SMART goals, let's distill these teachings into actionable steps that both coaches and athletes can take to enhance their mental toughness and guide their success on the green.

For the Coach

1. Promote Goal-Setting: Empower your athletes with the knowledge of harnessing the potential of setting both short-term and long-term goals. Make them aware that goal-setting is about directing attention and establishing meaningful targets, not just for the next game but for their overall growth as a golfer.

2. Guide Goal Prioritization: Assist your athletes in organizing their goals in order of importance. This will help them optimize their time and habits.

3. Stress the Importance of Writing Goals Down: Encourage your athletes to write down their goals. This simple act can solidify their commitment and improve their accountability.

4. Demonstrate the Different Types of Goals: Help your athletes comprehend the difference between process goals and outcome goals. Both types are important and can foster various facets of growth and skill development.

For the Athlete

1. Understand the Power of Goals: Embrace the crucial role that goals play in your golf journey. Understand that they serve as targets, not just for individual games, but for your broader skill development.

2. Apply the SMART Framework: When setting goals, make sure they are Specific, Measurable, Attainable, Realistic, and Time-sensitive. This framework can guide you to set meaningful and achievable targets.

3. Prioritize Your Goals: Organize your goals in order of importance to help manage your time and habits effectively.

4. Write Your Goals Down: Solidify your commitment to your goals by writing them down. It's a simple act that can help improve your accountability and focus.

5. Identify Your Process and Outcome Goals: Understand the difference between process goals, which focus on specific aspects of your golfing technique, and outcome goals, which are more concerned with the end results. Both types are important and contribute to your overall performance.

Remember, goal setting is not a one-time task, but an ongoing process that demands revisiting and refining. Embrace this process, and take comfort in the knowledge that the effort you put into setting the right goals can significantly shape your journey in golf. Enjoy the journey, and may each swing take you closer to your goals.

Conclusion

This chapter has underscored the essence of effective goal-setting. Drawing wisdom from Rory McIlroy's approach, we learned to structure our goals utilizing the SMART framework, distinguishing between short-term and long-term process and outcome goals. Importantly, we also discovered how setting the right goals not only drives success on the golf course but also fuels motivation and wards off failure in life. Justin Thomas's story served as a stirring exemplification of these principles. As we carry on our journey toward mastering mental toughness in golf, let's strive to set the right goals and diligently pursue them.

Chapter 7: Skill #6—Patience and Persistence

"Execute, execute, execute..." The phrase resonates, echoing down the fairway and rebounding back to where we stand. It's more than just a command. It's a mantra, an ethos for the game and life. These wise words come from none other than professional golfer J. L. Lewis. "If you are coming down the stretch in a tournament, and you have a chance to place high, I don't think about that. I think about this shot. What's the best I can do on this shot?" Lewis elucidates a fundamental truth about golf and about life itself. Success is not about the constant focus on winning or losing; it's about making ourselves better, one stroke at a time.

To truly understand the depth of Lewis's philosophy, we need to dive deeper into his career. Known for his unwavering resolve and quiet patience, Lewis has always been an ardent advocate of resilience in golf. He knew that to reach his goals, he needed to look beyond the immediate challenges, adopting a long-term perspective. This principle is a cornerstone in building mental toughness. As we delve further into this chapter, we will explore Lewis's journey, and how it encapsulates the essence of our sixth skill: patience and persistence.

Golf, more than any other sport, is a game of patience. Whether you're a novice player or a seasoned professional, the significance of patience can't be overstated. It's the delicate thread that weaves itself into every aspect of the game, affecting your swing, your shots, and how you deal with tough situations on the course. It dictates your rhythm, provides the courage to persist when nothing seems to be going your way, and, ultimately, fuels your journey of growth and improvement. In short, patience is what separates those who give up too early from those who stick it out.

Consider the case of Jordan Spieth, a phenomenal player whose impatience led to a pivotal decline in one of his scores. This anecdote serves as a compelling example of how patience, or lack thereof, can radically impact one's game. It's a testament to the fact that there's no point in practicing if you're not willing to do it over and over again. So, how do we cultivate patience? Much like the verdant greens we play on, patience requires consistent tending and care. It's about discipline, emotional self-control, and remembering why we play golf in the first place. Above all, patience is about showing up, again and again, despite the trials and tribulations we face.

Equally important to patience is persistence. The roller coaster of development in golf, or any aspect of life, is non-linear, filled with ups and downs. Mental toughness, which patience and persistence help build, allows us to endure and adapt to these fluctuations. It enables us to weather the storm when things fall apart and to keep going, not because we want to, but because it's hard.

This chapter explores numerous stories to inspire you, like that of Michael Thompson. Known for his extraordinary patience, Thompson focused on minimizing mistakes rather than striving for a perfect shot every time. His story underscores the tremendous power of patience and persistence, proving that these qualities truly pave the path to victory on and off the course.

In Chapter 7, we will look beyond the fairway, embrace the beauty of patience and the virtue of persistence. It's here that we unlock the secret to resilience and mental toughness. Let's embark on this journey together. One shot, one stroke, one step at a time. Remember, it's all about "Execute, execute, execute..."

How Patience Affects Your Game

There's an old saying that "golf is a game of inches." In reality, it is a game that demands patience above all else. Golf, in its essence, isn't just a test of skill and strategy but also a testament to patience. Every player, new or veteran, learns that the sport is a prolonged engagement, not just with the course and the ball but with one's own mindset. Whether you're fighting the frustration of a bunker shot or the nervousness of a lead, patience can make the difference between a round that is well-played and one that is riddled with errors.

For novice players, the challenge can seem daunting. The rules, the techniques, and the sheer breadth of things to learn could make you want to throw in the towel. But it's patience that helps you see beyond the struggle, embrace the process, and, most importantly, evolve with every swing.

The Value of Patience in Practice and Execution

The essence of practice lies not just in repetition but in resilience. It's about doing it over and over again, even when the initial outcomes aren't promising. As a golfer, you need the patience to persist through the painstaking process of refining your shots and improving your game.

Patience isn't just about perseverance. It's about maintaining your cool when things get tricky. In situations like the dreaded bunker shot, patience is what keeps you from making hasty, ill-thought decisions. It gives you the mental space to evaluate your options, think strategically, and navigate out of tight spots. In this sense, patience governs not just your swing but also your overall game management, affecting how you handle tough situations, maintain your rhythm, and even deal with bad luck.

Lessons from the Pros: The Tale of Jordan Spieth

Sometimes, the best lessons come from real-life examples. The story of Jordan Spieth at the Masters serves as a stark reminder of how patience, or lack thereof, can sway a golf game.

As Spieth neared the finish line at the Masters, he was leading and on course for a historic victory. Then, suddenly, his rhythm faltered. Two bad shots, and his game was disrupted. His lack of patience got the better of him, causing him to rush his putts and make costly errors. The lead slipped away, and so did the tournament.

Spieth's experience illustrates the potentially game-changing impact of patience. Had he maintained his calm and not rushed, the final result might have been different. His story underscores the importance of having patience not just during practice or in the face of obstacles but, crucially, in handling pressure and high-stakes situations.

How to Nurture Patience in Golf

Building patience is a mindful process. Begin with awareness. Identify what triggers impatience in you. Maybe it's a missed putt or a wrong decision. Recognize these triggers and plan how you'll manage them next time. Develop a forward-looking mindset. Don't let one bad hole or shot define the rest of your game. Golf is a marathon, not a sprint. Keep your focus on the remaining holes rather than dwelling on past mistakes.

Maintain a steady routine. Resist the urge to rush or make hasty decisions, especially when you're feeling pressured. A consistent pace not only enhances your performance but also keeps your mind calm, helping you stay patient throughout the game.

Golf is indeed a game of patience. The sport teaches you to balance the quest for perfection with the acceptance of imperfection. As every golfer knows, the road to improvement isn't always straight or smooth. It's a journey marked by constant learning, unlearning, and relearning, and patience is the fuel that drives this journey.

Strengthening Your Mind by Never Giving Up

Building mental toughness is a complex journey, much like an expedition into an unknown forest. This journey is a crucial part of life, especially for adolescents, where the seeds of mental toughness planted early can pave the way for strong, resilient adult life. Parents, too, play a significant role in shaping the mental landscape of their children. Strengthening one's mind through patience and persistence can enhance mental toughness and provide a useful toolbox for navigating the sometimes-turbulent waters of life.

Patience and Persistence: The Cornerstones of a Strong Mindset

The secret to strengthening one's mind often lies in the seemingly ordinary virtues of patience and persistence. Patience, in particular, forms the bedrock of building mental toughness. It requires a blend of discipline, focus, and a deep understanding of delayed gratification. Just as a top athlete wouldn't leap into an elite training program without first mastering the basics, it's essential for everyone, especially teens, to cultivate patience in their lives.

Persistence, on the other hand, is the stubborn companion that keeps us moving forward. Imagine you're in a dark tunnel; persistence is the unwavering belief that there's light at the end, even if you can't see it yet. It encourages you to keep taking steps forward, even when progress seems elusive. Together, patience and persistence make a formidable team. Like two sides of a coin, they complement each other. Where patience urges you to wait for the right moment, persistence pushes you to keep striving for your goals. This synergy is particularly important when riding the roller coaster of personal development and growth. Progress isn't linear. It's full of ups and downs, victories and setbacks, growth spurts, and stagnant phases. It's during these turbulent times that the combined power of patience and persistence shines through.

In the same vein, motivation alone isn't enough to build mental toughness. It's like a spark. While it may ignite the fire, it can't sustain it. You need the steady fuel of patience and persistence when the going gets tough. These traits will keep you grounded, reminding you to hold on even when your goals seem out of reach.

Patience and persistence are like the endurance athletes of your mental toolbox. They're not glamorous and they don't demand attention, but they're indispensable. They're the stamina that keeps the camera of your focus steady, the discipline that holds everything in place during the storms of life. By consistently exercising these traits, you strengthen your mental muscle, not only as a physical capacity but also as a proof of your resilience to past adversities. Remember, there will be times when you're required to do something not because you want to, but because it's necessary. It's in these moments that patience and persistence come to the fore, ensuring that you're mentally equipped to meet these challenges head-on.

Patience, persistence, and perspective are like three unwavering lighthouses guiding you through the tumultuous seas of life. They remind you that the most valuable things take time, that hard work and tenacity pay off, and that maintaining a broader perspective of your journey is crucial. They're not just tools to be used in times of distress but habits to be cultivated, nurtured, and embedded in your everyday life.

Stories to Inspire: Minimizing Mistakes With Patience

In the riveting world of professional golf, a single shot can make the difference between victory and defeat. Many rising stars have lost their sheen in the face of such pressure, failing to close in crucial moments. However, there are those who conquer this immense challenge through a remarkable virtue: patience. This was the path Michael Thompson chose to tread, which led to his success.

Michael Thompson, a seasoned player on the PGA Tour, was known more for his struggles than for his victories. For years, he had been battling fiercely to maintain his standing among the world's top-tier players. While others faltered in the face of immense pressure, Thompson found a key to success: patience. This virtue, combined with his skillful putting, led to a triumphant breakthrough, breaking his winless streak.

Thompson opened the TPC Twin Cities tournament with a flawless round, hitting all 18 greens and sinking almost 100 feet of putts. He played a conservative game, sticking to his plan, capitalizing on his strengths in iron play and putting and minimizing errors. It was not just about hitting every shot perfectly; it was about staying patient, playing to his strengths, and capitalizing on opportunities when they arose. Using V1 Game's Analysis function, we find that Thompson's stellar performance stemmed from his iron play and putting skills. He only made three bogeys during the entire week, tied for the fewest in the field. However, Thompson's conservative strategy paid off—he lost less than a third of a stroke, on average, with the driver.

The artificial intelligence of V1 Game's Virtual Coach analyzed Thompson's weekend performance, underscoring his ability to reach his potential by reducing errors. He committed just one three-putt and one penalty throughout the four-day event, scoring an average of 66.3. The AI suggested that he could shave off even more strokes with fewer mistakes, potentially averaging a score of 65.

Thompson's strategy might not seem glamorous. It lacked high-risk, high-reward shots, focusing instead on consistency and precision. Yet it was this cautious, meticulous approach that allowed him to excel. By relying on his iron play and putting, Thompson played to his strengths and minimized his mistakes.

One lesson that teens and parents can take from Thompson's story is the power of patience. It can be tempting to aim for glory with every shot, but often, success comes from knowing your strengths and playing a steady game. In a world that often prioritizes speed and immediate results, Thompson's journey reminds us that patience, persistence, and strategic thinking can lead to the greatest victories.

Teeing Up: Actionable Steps to Improve Mental Toughness

For the Coach

1. Promote Mindful Practice: Use the story of J. L. Lewis to emphasize the importance of patience and focusing on the current shot rather than on the overall outcome of the game.

2. Highlight the Impact of Patience: Using the resources provided, explain how patience influences not just the swing but also the shots and the player's ability to handle difficult situations.

3. Present Real-Life Consequences: Discuss the example of Jordan Spieth to show how a lack of patience can negatively impact a player's score.

4. Guide Emotional Self-Control: Train your athletes in emotional self-control, a crucial skill that helps them remain patient even when things aren't going their way.

5. Encourage Persistence: Teach your athletes about the nonlinear nature of improvement and progress. Emphasize that motivation isn't enough; they need persistence and patience when things don't go according to plan.

For the Athlete

1. Embrace the Journey: Remember that golf is a long-term journey. Be patient with your progress and persistent in your practice. Understand that improvement may not be linear, and be prepared for ups and downs.

2. Prioritize Consistency: Show up for practice consistently. It's not about perfecting a skill in one session but rather about improving gradually over time.

3. Emotional Self-Control: Practice emotional self-control.

When things seem to be going off the rails, take a step back, breathe, and be patient.

4. Identify Your Triggers: Recognize what makes you impatient on the course. Is it a missed shot, a high-stakes situation, or pressure from opponents? Once you're aware of these triggers, you can work on strategies to manage your reactions better.

5. Be Inspired: Take inspiration from Michael Thompson. His patience and strategy of minimizing mistakes rather than trying to hit every shot perfectly could be a helpful approach to emulate in your own game.

Conclusion

This chapter outlines the profound importance of patience and persistence in golf, encapsulating the philosophies of professional golfers such as J. L. Lewis and Michael Thompson. The golf course serves as an arena that vividly mirrors the ebb and flow of life's challenges, teaching us the power of resilience and mental toughness. As seen in the case of Jordan Spieth, a lack of patience can disrupt the rhythm of the game, leading to costly errors. On the other hand, Thompson's tale underscores the benefits of a patient and conservative approach, minimizing mistakes and leveraging personal strengths. The chapter affirms that golf is more than a game; it is a journey of self-improvement, urging us to persist through trials and adapt with every swing, mirroring the ebbs and flows of life itself. Patience and persistence are not merely instrumental to mastering the game; they are vital skills that strengthen our mental fortitude, preparing us for life's many challenges.

Chapter 8: Skill #7—Bouncing Back from Failure

"Failure," Phil Mickelson once confessed, "has always been my greatest motivator." These words, emerging from one of golf's most celebrated figures, encapsulate a truth intrinsic not only to the game of golf but to every endeavor that demands unwavering resilience. This chapter is about bouncing back from failure, about the rocky roads and stumbled steps that form the pathway to mastery in golf, and perhaps, in life itself.

From the meticulously manicured greens of Augusta to the windswept links of St Andrews, failure is as ubiquitous in golf as the clubs themselves. There's no golfer, amateur or professional, who hasn't tasted the bitter sting of a missed putt, an errant drive, or a dismal scorecard. Yet, within these crushing moments lies the crux of our conversation—the transformative power of failure. It is in these instances of setback, when the crowd's applause fades into a disquieting silence, that a golfer's resilience is truly tested.

Everyone fails. Jack Nicklaus, Arnold Palmer, Tiger Woods—every luminary of the fairways has weathered storms of disappointment and defeat. However, the essence of their greatness lies not in the absence of failure, but in their responses to it. It's not the crumbling under pressure that defines us, but the audacity to rise from the dust and take another swing. Indeed, the specter of failure looms large, especially in a sport as public and scrutinized as golf. Many golfers fear failing, not just for their professional reputation, but for the perceived embarrassment, the imaginary spotlight that illuminates their shortcomings. However, understanding and accepting this fear is the first step toward altering our perspective on failure.

Every golfer, in fact, every individual striving for improvement, needs failure. It is through the lens of our missteps that we perceive our areas of improvement, distinguishing between luck-based success and skill-driven triumph. It's through failure that we gain insights into our game, that we forge our path to betterment. This isn't about romanticizing failure, but rather about recognizing its inherent value as a learning tool.

But how do we conquer failure? How do we mold it into a stepping stone rather than a stumbling block? The key lies in a potent blend of self-awareness, goal-setting, and persistent patience. We must understand our failures, dissecting them to pinpoint their roots, while also focusing on our strengths. Our aspirations should be grounded in reality, encouraging consistent progress rather than unreachable perfection. Above all, we must arm ourselves with patience, knowing that true resilience takes time to cultivate.

Let's take a moment to delve into the incredible journey of James Hahn. Here was a man who once swapped his clubs for shoe sales, his dreams of professional golf seeming an unattainable mirage. Yet, failure was not his finale. He not only clawed his way back into the game, but also ascended to the summit of a PGA Tour victory. His story is not just about success, but more importantly, about resilience in the face of failure.

In the rest of the chapter, we will delve deeper into the heart of failure, unraveling its complexities and exploring its potent influence on our performance. Engaging in this dialogue may not be effortless, yet it remains an imperative discourse. After all, to quote the legendary Phil Mickelson once more: "I am motivated by failure. I work harder because of failure." And so should we all.

The Truth About Failure

The truth about failure is that it is a universal phenomenon, an essential component in the journey of growth and success. It's the hidden, yet indispensable ingredient of any feat of achievement, be it in sports, business, or life in general. It's particularly crucial to remember that in sports, no player is without failure—it's an inevitable part of the game. This includes golf, where even the greatest players have their share of failures.

Take, for instance, golf legends like Rory McIlroy, Tiger Woods, or Bubba Watson. They've all had their fair share of failures. McIlroy, despite being a two-time major winner, had a year of considerable disappointment where he performed significantly below his potential. Tiger Woods, arguably the greatest golfer of all time, had a drought of five years without winning a major, which, by his high standards, was seen as a failure. And Bubba Watson, following his spectacular win at the Masters in 2012, has struggled to reclaim the same form, marking a downward trajectory in his career.

Failure is a pervasive reality—everyone fails. However, the defining aspect isn't the failure itself but the response to it. What truly matters is the subsequent action when failure strikes: the rebound, the lessons learned, and the resilience displayed. It's in these moments of failure that characters are tested, skills are refined, and greatness is born.

Relationship Between Failure and Fear

Let's delve a bit deeper into the relationship between failure and fear. Many golfers, indeed many people in general, are afraid of failing. The fear of appearing inadequate, of making mistakes, and of looking silly in front of others can be a significant hindrance to one's performance. This fear is often exacerbated by the Spotlight Effect—a psychological phenomenon where people tend to believe they are being observed and judged more critically than they actually are. This fear can be paralyzing, making people shy away from risks and challenges that could potentially lead to their growth and improvement.

Understanding this fear and the Spotlight Effect can, however, be the first step toward changing how we perceive failure. When we recognize that we are not constantly under intense scrutiny and judgment as we think, the fear of failure and of looking silly diminishes. This realization can free us from the chains of fear, enabling us to take bold strides, make mistakes, and learn from them without undue anxiety. Furthermore, viewing failure as an opportunity to learn and grow rather than as a humiliating defeat can transform our relationship with it. Failure then becomes not an end but a stepping-stone on the path to improvement and eventual success. This shift in perception can be incredibly empowering, making us more resilient, determined, and successful in the long run, both on the golf course and in life.

Why Every Golfer Needs Failure

In the realm of golf, as in life, failure is an inevitable companion. The game, in its unpredictable beauty, teaches us that no matter how adept we become at wielding our clubs, there's always a chance for an unexpected turn of events. A perfect swing might still result in a bad bounce. And as we come to understand this intrinsic unpredictability, we realize that golf is more about influence than control, a continuous negotiation with circumstances that, at times, refuse to align with our intentions.

There is an intrinsic power in failure that all golfers, whether seasoned professionals or enthusiastic teenagers, need to harness. In a competitive match, only one golfer can emerge victorious; the rest must face their own shortcomings. Failure isn't just a possibility in golf–it's built into the fabric of the game.

But why is failure so crucial? Why must every golfer experience it? For one, failure is the most efficient teacher we can encounter on our path to mastery. It guides us to recognize our flaws and strive for improvement. Failure serves as a mirror reflecting back our weaknesses, not to discourage us, but to indicate where our focus should lie. It is through failure that we learn to differentiate between areas that require attention and those that are already well-honed.

It's a Matter of How You Look at Failure

This transformative aspect of failure is highly contingent on how we perceive it. Like a prism splitting light, failure can hurt or help, depending on the angle from which we view it. To the discouraged eye, it can appear as a stinging setback. However, to the resilient eye, failure transforms into an invaluable learning opportunity.

The choice, therefore, is yours. You can allow failure to deflate your morale, or you can wield it as a tool for self-improvement. If you let failure use you, it can lead to self-doubt, frustration, and stagnation. Conversely, using failure to your advantage can fuel progress, sharpen your skills, and ultimately elevate your game. Moreover, consistent success can create an illusion of perfection, leaving no room for growth. It's the hard knocks that bring balance and offer insights on how to enhance performance. If you're always winning, you may never discern the need to improve. Therefore, failure becomes a reality check, a reminder that there's always a path toward refinement.

At times, even when success is achieved, it may be due to a lucky break rather than skill. It's crucial to acknowledge that luck, unlike skill, isn't repeatable or dependable. Failure, however, guides us to identify and correct our mistakes, enhancing our ability to succeed without the crutch of luck. Reframing failure as an opportunity rather than a setback allows it to become our time machine. It provides us with an outlook to revisit our past performance, analyze it, and then utilize those lessons to shape a better future in the game. This shift in perspective is integral to personal and golfing growth.

While it's true that golf can knock you down, it's equally true that it gives you the opportunity to rise again, stronger and wiser. Embracing an "acceptance first" attitude toward failure not only helps you bounce back faster but also encourages mental resilience. The ability to let go of past mistakes and focus on future potential is a valuable lesson, one that extends beyond the golf course and into life.

Remember, as a golfer, every missed shot, every bad round, is a stepping stone toward your best self. Every failure is a lesson, a signpost pointing the way to improvement. As you learn to accept and embrace failure, you'll begin to see each misstep not as a defeat but as an opportunity to grow, to learn, and, ultimately, to succeed.

How to Conquer Failure

Golf, in all its verdant glory, offers a rare confluence of mental and physical challenges, where each stroke represents a battle against ourselves and the course. Indeed, the game's nature embodies the principle of imperfection. Even the legends of golf like Tiger Woods and Ben Hogan have won only a fraction of their matches at the start of their career. This humbling fact brings us to one crucial understanding: learning to conquer failure is as vital as mastering the swing.

As the age-old adage suggests, "Everyone has a plan until they get punched in the mouth." Failure on the golf course can be that punch. It's how you respond that distinguishes the resilient from the rest.

Recognize the Specificity of Failure

A missed putt or a shanked drive—these are common hiccups in any golfer's career, be they novice or pro. But remember, failure in golf is specific. It's an error in one aspect of the game and not a reflection of your overall ability. Poor performance on the driving range doesn't automatically doom you to a bad round on the course. Instead, focus on transforming each failure into an opportunity for growth and improvement.

Unearth the Roots of Failure

To deal with failure effectively, you need to identify its causes. The vagaries of the course, an unexpected gust of wind, or a momentary lapse in concentration can all conspire to produce a less-than-desirable result. The key here is not to control your environment but to tune into it, fully absorbing and adapting to its challenges. Embrace the unpredictability, revel in the complexity, and accept that some factors are simply beyond your control.

Realistic Goals

All pro golfers have one thing in common: they set achievable and realistic goals. It's about understanding your capabilities and setting targets that stretch your abilities without setting yourself up for inevitable failure. Your goals should inspire progress, not breed frustration. Keep them flexible, accommodating for growth, and remember that small, incremental improvements often lead to significant long-term gains.

Celebrate Your Strengths

While it's important to work on your weaknesses, do not forget to play to your strengths. In the struggle to overcome our shortcomings, we sometimes overlook our assets. Remember, the road to success is not paved solely with rectified errors. Use your strengths as your secret weapon to balance out your weaknesses and gain an edge.

Patience, Persistence, and Practice

The three pillars of Patience, Persistence, and Practice, often referred to as the three P's, form the foundation for overcoming setbacks and failures in the realm of golf. Give yourself enough room to fail and learn from those failures. Persistence allows you to keep trying, even when progress seems slow or non-existent. Practice, the act of deliberate repetition, helps cement new skills and strategies.

Learning to handle failure is not an easy feat, but it is a rewarding one. Adopting these strategies used by pro golfers can help young golfers and their parents navigate the trials of this beautiful game with grace and resilience. Remember, every golfer has faced failure, and every golfer has the capacity to bounce back from it. The ability to conquer failure is the hidden ninth club in every golfer's bag, ready to be deployed when things don't go as planned. The challenge is not in avoiding failure but in learning how to dance with it.

Stories to Inspire: From Designer Shoes to Greens—The Unlikely Journey of James Hahn

In a stark departure from his desired path, James Hahn found himself not treading the manicured golf turfs, but tracing the steps of high-end fashion labels like Jimmy Choo and Christian Louboutin. His professional golf aspirations were seemingly on hold while he supplemented his income by vending luxury footwear in two Nordstrom outlets in Northern California.

Hahn's climb to accomplishment took an unconventional route. After his academic journey at Cal-Berkeley, he explored an array of professions. These included being a real estate representative, a mortgage intermediary, and a junior account executive at a marketing firm. While these roles sustained his financial needs, they failed to fulfill the longing for the sport he had adored since his early years.

While working at Nordstrom, Hahn's charisma and diligence earned him the admiration of both his colleagues and customers. Yet, beneath his sunny disposition, a dream still simmered, one that he had put on hold after quitting the Cal golf team before his senior year due to other priorities. However, the triumph of his former teammates in the NCAA championship, an event he had missed out on, was the spark Hahn needed. "I was not going to let my senior year define my golfing career. It was just another chapter in the book," Hahn declared. This was his wake-up call. He was ready for his next chapter.

Financial constraints led Hahn to leave golf again, this time for a job at West Advertising. His position there, he recounts, was one of the toughest yet most enriching of his professional experiences. Despite the taxing nature of his work, Hahn was honing an essential skill—meticulous attention to detail.

The desire to rekindle his golf career led Hahn back to Nordstroms. This time he was selling shoes, a job that surprisingly provided him with more income and a flexible schedule for his practice sessions. As the seasons changed and the weather improved, Hahn knew it was time. He submitted his notice and said, "I need to get back into playing golf."

This marked a turning point in Hahn's journey. His reentry into the world of golf was not a smooth sail. It took several years playing in Korea, Canada, and the Web.com Tour before he finally tasted victory. His triumph, along with his charming "Gangnam Style" dance that went viral on YouTube, put Hahn back on the map.

His friend Joe Brazell believes in Hahn's potential. He sees Hahn's journey, with its twists and turns, as the foundation for future success. "His personality, he has an amazing work ethic and when you combine that with how talented he is and his ability to remain positive... it's a recipe for success," Brazell comments. Despite his significant million-dollar triumph, Hahn maintains a grounded and humble demeanor. He's happy to be a "Foot Locker kind of person" and doesn't see his past jobs as embarrassments but as learning experiences. He values the hardships he faced because they remind him of the beauty of his current life.

Hahn's narrative stands as a testament to the strength of resilience, the significance of diligent effort, and the essence of staying authentic to one's true self. His unconventional journey is a reminder to both teens and parents alike that it's never too late to pursue a dream, and that success isn't always achieved by following a straight line.

Teeing Up: Actionable Steps to Improve Mental Toughness

For the Coach

1. Normalize Failure: Use the quote from Phil Mickelson and his experiences to demonstrate that even the greatest athletes face failures. Emphasize that failure is a part of the journey, not an endpoint.

2. Shift the Perspective on Failure: Utilize examples from famous golfers who faced significant failures and yet bounced back. Teach your players that failure is not to be feared but to be embraced as a learning opportunity.

3. Create a Safe Space for Failure: Establish an environment where players feel safe to make mistakes and can learn from them without judgment. Remind them of the Spotlight Effect, where they might think everyone is watching their failures, while in reality, most people are too focused on their own performance.

4. Transform Failure into Success: Encourage your players to view failures as stepping stones to success. Teach them to differentiate between the aspects of the game to focus on and those to ignore, using failure as an indicator.

5. Promote Resilience: Instill in your players that it's not the failure that defines them but how they respond to it. Use the story of James Hahn as an inspiring example of bouncing back.

For the Athlete

1. Embrace Failure: Understand that every golfer, including the pros, fails. Rather than fearing failure, use it as a means to improve.

2. Learn from Failure: Each failure provides valuable lessons about your game. Use these lessons to work on your weaknesses and refine your strengths.

3. Identify the Cause: When failure occurs, analyze the factors that led to it, including those beyond your control. This understanding will enable you to devise strategies to handle similar situations in the future.

4. Set Realistic Goals: Having achievable and realistic goals can help you manage failure. Revisit your goals regularly and adjust them based on your progress and performance.

5. Balance Patience with Persistence: Remember that improving your game is a process that requires both patience and persistence. Allow yourself room to fail, but also remain dedicated to your practice and continuous improvement.

Conclusion

Failure is not a verdict, but a vital step on the journey of self-improvement, both in golf and in life. Embracing the inevitability of failure can liberate us from the fear of defeat, enabling us to boldly embrace challenges and risks that drive growth. Recognizing failure as a specific, isolated incident rather than as a sweeping judgment of our abilities can prevent us from being paralyzed by fear. Moreover, understanding the difference between being in control and having influence, setting realistic goals, celebrating strengths, and practicing patience, persistence, and deliberate practice can help us rise from the ashes of failure stronger and wiser. As the unique journey of James Hahn reminds us, there is no straightforward path to success. Everyone experiences setbacks and detours, but it's our resilience, hard work, and authenticity that ultimately steer us to our goals. As golfers, or indeed as individuals striving in any walk of life, it's crucial to remember that every failure is a stepping stone toward growth, a signpost directing us to improvement, and a reminder that there's always a way to enhance our performance.

CHAPTER 9: SKILL #8—PRACTICING POSITIVITY

"If you don't like it, then you're not going to be here very long. So, learn to embrace it and enjoy it. When I first came across these inspiring words by Jordan Spieth, I couldn't help but reflect on the power of positivity and the role it plays in golf. How, I wondered, does a golfer remain positive, especially when faced with intimidating shots and challenging holes? How do we apply this positivity not just to the game of golf but also to our everyday lives?

In 2017, Spieth, despite his already remarkable career, faced a prolonged slump. Some were quick to pronounce the end of his golfing prowess. However, the resolute golfer, imbued with an iron-clad sense of mental fortitude, fought through adversity. He shifted his perspective, choosing to focus on the positive aspects of his game rather than dwell on his losses. His resolve and positivity culminated in a triumphant comeback, underscoring the importance of mental strength in golf.

This chapter will delve deeper into the concept of positivity, a critical skill in the armory of any golfer. However, before we proceed, we need to debunk a few myths.

The first is the so-called Positivity Myth, a widespread misconception that positivity is all about ignoring the negatives and solely focusing on the positives. Many believe that they can will their way to a positive outcome. Unfortunately, it's not that simple. Neither negative emotions nor difficult circumstances are entities to be ignored or avoided. Instead, they are a part of the golfing journey to be embraced and learned from.

The second fallacy we need to dispel is about the nature of positive thinking. It is not a matter of shifting away from negative thoughts but rather about reinterpreting them in a more constructive light. I'd argue that it's better to describe it as "neutral thinking"—a term that speaks to an objective approach to the way things are. We'll explore this concept further, discussing how it ties into self-belief and confidence and focusing on the elements within our control.

But why is positivity so important in golf? Simple: Positivity serves as a calming force, shapes your overall mindset, and has a profound impact on how you perceive and approach the game. It possesses the power to propel your vision and enhance your focus on the course. Conversely, negative thinking not only sabotages your game but also affects those around you and dampens the fun of playing. It's a self-perpetuating cycle–poor shots reinforce negative thoughts, which lead to more poor shots.

But how do we practice positivity? I'd like to share some tips for fostering a positive mindset both on and off the course. First and foremost, set your intentions before the game. Like aiming, focus on where you want to go and what you want to achieve. Visualization plays a crucial role here, as envisioning success not only makes it more likely but also boosts your confidence. Even negative emotions can be used productively as an opportunity to analyze, evaluate, and improve.

One of the most inspiring stories of positivity in golf is that of Ally McDonald. Despite battling negative thoughts and self-doubt, McDonald used positive thinking to propel herself to a win. She is a living testament to the transformative power of positivity.

This chapter aims to inspire you, to reveal the power of positivity, and to equip you with the tools to apply it to your game and life. Always bear in mind that the ultimate objective is to derive enjoyment from the game. Positivity, without a doubt, serves as a vital step in that direction. So, let's embrace the challenge and enjoy the journey together!

The Positivity Myth

The Positivity Myth and the misconceptions surrounding positive thinking form a crucial part of today's dialogue about mental and emotional well-being. The notion that positivity is simply about emphasizing the good and disregarding the bad is a fallacy that needs to be debunked, particularly when considering the psyche of teenagers.

Positive thinking, contrary to popular belief, is not a magic wand that can simply be waved to conjure a favorable outcome. Instead, it is a mindset, a perspective that encompasses a more comprehensive and nuanced understanding of life's complexities. It involves acknowledging the difficulties and challenges we face, not glossing over them. Many have misunderstood it to be an elimination of all negativity, which is both unrealistic and unhelpful. Positive thinking has its merits. It can serve as a motivational force, a catalyst to initiate a project or an endeavor. However, like a discount coupon, it's only a portion of the success equation. It's valuable, yes, but without the necessary resources, effort, and resilience, success remains out of reach. Simply put, you cannot will your way to success by positive thinking alone.

Negative Emotions are Not Always Bad

The perception that positivity should be a constant state of being is another fallacy. Life, by its very nature, is a mixed bag of experiences—some good, others not so much. Attempting to maintain an unfaltering facade of positivity can lead to a denial of negative emotions. It is essential to remind ourselves, and especially our young ones, that it's okay not to be okay sometimes. Emotions, regardless of their nature, play a vital role in our personal growth and understanding of self.

Negative emotion is not the villain it's often painted to be. It isn't something that should be shunned or ignored. Ancient societies understood this, exposing their young to trials designed to prepare them for life's unpredictable twists and turns. In today's culture, where optimism is highly praised, this notion may seem alien. However, confronting these negative emotions can indeed be beneficial, enabling us to explore new dimensions of our personality and emotional resilience.

The concept of a positive image, particularly in the age of social media, is a breeding ground for the disparity between perception and reality. Profiles teeming with uplifting affirmations, success stories, and tales of unbridled joy can paint a picture that's far removed from the complexities of real life. There's a danger in perceiving these "positivity-only" individuals as paragons of happiness, often overlooking the reality that they, too, face challenges and struggles.

Finally, positivity doesn't mandate an eternally cheerful outlook in every sphere of life. Just like the aroma of freshly ground coffee can inspire positivity one weekend, the loud grinder or a lack of milk the next weekend may lead to frustration. These are natural fluctuations in our mood and emotions, influenced by myriad factors such as weather, hormones, or other people's moods. Accepting these variations as part of the human experience is a healthier and more realistic approach than striving for unwavering positivity.

In essence, cultivating a healthy mindset involves not just the capacity for positivity but also the courage to confront and understand our negative emotions. It's about striking a balance and navigating the ups and downs of life with resilience and grace, not about suppressing the hard parts. This is the message we need to relay to our teenagers and their parents alike: that positivity is a tool, not a destination, and it is only one of many that we need to live fulfilling, balanced lives.

What Positive Thinking Really Is

Positive thinking, in its authentic essence, is not about cultivating a relentless optimism that ignores the darker aspects of life. Rather, it is a balanced approach to processing life's events, which involves confronting both positive and negative experiences and finding constructive ways to respond to them.

One of the most lucid examples of this balance can be found in the world of sports, particularly golf. This game, often considered a mind sport, is rife with ups and downs, highs and lows, and victories and defeats. The act of playing golf is not just about physically hitting the ball; it's also about mentally preparing for the swing, accepting the outcome, and strategizing for the next move.

Reframing Negative Thoughts in a Positive Light

Instead of trying to suppress negative thoughts or feelings of failure, a more effective approach is to reframe them. For example, instead of viewing a missed shot as a failure, see it as an opportunity to learn and improve. It's about putting a positive spin on things, not about pretending that everything is perpetually rosy. This isn't to say that one should revel in failure, but rather to accept it as part of the journey and to find lessons in it that will contribute to future successes.

Embracing Neutral Thinking

This concept aligns with what can be termed "neutral thinking:" an objective, realistic approach to situations. It doesn't force positivity or negativity but instead takes a step back, viewing circumstances as they truly are. Neutral thinking involves focusing on what is within one's control instead of being preoccupied with the desired outcome. It bolsters self-belief and confidence, empowering individuals to believe in their abilities to handle challenges and make the most of opportunities.

Neutral Thinking in Action

Applying this to golf, neutral thinking could involve a golfer acknowledging that they're having a bad day on the course. Still, instead of spiraling into negativity or forcing unfounded optimism, they remind themselves that everyone has off days. They would then refocus on the aspects of the game that are within their control: their breathing, their grip, their swing, and their mindset. In another instance, if a golfer hits the ball into the rough, instead of panicking or getting frustrated, neutral thinking would encourage them to calmly assess the situation, think about their options, and strategize their next shot based on the realities of their position.

Neutral thinking can be applied to various situations in life, not just golf. For instance, a teenager who receives a lower grade than expected might initially feel disappointed. Neutral thinking would guide them to accept this reality, reflect on areas of improvement, and put in the necessary effort to achieve better results next time. Similarly, parents dealing with challenging situations at work or at home can also adopt neutral thinking by focusing on the controllable aspects of the situation and navigating through it with a realistic and balanced mindset.

In essence, neutral thinking is about accepting life's highs and lows and taking an objective, solution-focused approach. This mindset is more sustainable and realistic than a positivity-only approach and helps cultivate resilience, self-belief, and a balanced outlook on life. It is a skill that can help teenagers and parents alike navigate the complexities of life more effectively.

How Positivity Pays off in Golf

We all know that wishing doesn't automatically lead to success, especially in a sport as technical and complex as golf. Still, the power of a positive mindset is not to be underestimated. It's not about celebrating when you find yourself in a bunker, or trying to convince yourself that a less than ideal outcome is great. Rather, it's about acknowledging your present reality and developing a positive strategy for your next move. In golf, as in life, cultivating a positive mindset can significantly reduce anxiety and improve decision-making, setting you up for greater success on the course.

Framing Your Mindset: The Power of Positive Thinking

The beauty of our mind lies in its ability to envision. You control how you perceive a given situation, whether it's a doomed scenario or a golden opportunity. If you're the kind of golfer who constantly worries about possible mishaps, you're more likely to steer your ball toward trouble. But did you know that you can train your brain to visualize success rather than potential pitfalls? This is where the power of positive thinking truly comes into play.

As you prepare for your shot, picture the stroke you want to execute, not the mistakes you're anxious about making. Dwelling on the flaws in your swing will only produce more of the same unwanted moves. Conversely, if you visualize your club moving through the ball exactly as you'd like it to, your body will strive to make that vision a reality.

The Ripple Effects of Negativity: Golf, Mindset, and Relationships

The impact of your mindset extends far beyond your personal performance—it can also influence those around you. Negative thinking, particularly on the golf course, cannot only compromise your game but can also dampen the spirits of your fellow players. Consistently poor shots, often the result of a negative mindset, only serve to reinforce negative thoughts. These downbeat attitudes can prevent everyone, including yourself, from actually enjoying the game.

Ultimately, the essence of playing golf—or any sport, for that matter—should be to have fun. If you can't find enjoyment in your game, it begs the question: what's the point of playing? Golf, like life, should be an exciting journey, not a chore laden with stress and negativity.

Reclaiming the Joy of Golf: The Role of Positive Thinking

Golf is a game of mentality and attitude as much as it is about physical skill and precision. A positive mindset doesn't magically appear when you step onto the course—it needs to be consciously cultivated beforehand. By approaching your game with a positive attitude, you set yourself up for improved shots, increased enjoyment, and perhaps even a better relationship with your fellow golfers.

Pre-round positivity is crucial. Before the round even begins, try to instill in yourself the belief that you're going to have a good day. Nervous about that first tee shot? Don't be. Picture yourself landing a perfect shot right in the middle of the fairway, and work to turn that vision into reality. Maintaining a positive mindset even after a bad shot is vital for sustained success. Negative thinking often leads to a vicious cycle where one bad shot precipitates another. Instead, learn to let go of past mistakes and concentrate solely on the present shot.

Similarly, when you're on the putting green, confidence is key. Doubts can be as destructive as a sand trap, causing you to lose focus and miss putts that you're capable of making. Banish that uncertainty from your mind and believe in your ability to sink the putt. Lastly, remember to have fun. Golf is a wonderful game—one of the best, in fact. There's no room for frustration in such a beautiful sport. Embrace the experience, enjoy yourself, and let the good times (and great shots) roll. The positivity you bring to the course will likely spread to those around you, creating a more enjoyable experience for all involved. After all, isn't that what golf is all about?

Tricking Yourself Into Thinking Positively

Golf, like any sport, is a mental game. The key to success isn't solely in mastering physical skills but also in harnessing the power of your mind. This section explores practical ways you can cultivate a positive mindset, which can significantly enhance your performance on the fairway.

Aim for Your Target

Golf exemplifies precision and concentration. Prior to taking a shot, it's natural to be cautious of the hazards that lie ahead. However, focusing on the bunkers or water bodies often leads to negative anticipation, making it more likely for you to land in these very places. Instead, redirect your attention to where you want your ball to end up: the fairway or the green. By focusing on the desired outcome rather than potential pitfalls, you are mentally setting up a pathway for your body to follow, thus increasing your likelihood of a successful shot.

Focusing on Achieving Goals

Having a clear vision of what you want to accomplish is vital. Visualization is a powerful tool used by professional athletes worldwide. For every shot you're about to take, form a mental image of the swing you want to make, the trajectory you want the ball to follow, and the exact spot you want your ball to land. This visualization creates a blueprint in your mind, setting up a positive intention for success and priming your body to perform as you've mentally rehearsed.

Monitoring Your Self-Talk off the Course

It's important to remember that your inner dialogue doesn't only impact you during the game but also influences your mindset off the course. Endeavor to keep your self-talk positive and empowering, reminding yourself of your capabilities and progress. When you're away from the course, refrain from dwelling on past mistakes or missed targets. Instead, see every new game as a fresh start, an opportunity for growth and improvement.

Visualizing Success

The act of visualization, or mental rehearsal, is a proven method for improving performance in sports. Golf is no exception. Before every shot, take a moment to close your eyes and picture your perfect swing, the exact contact with the ball, and the ball gliding smoothly toward your target. This mental imagery serves to prepare your mind for the success that is about to follow. It also instills a sense of self-assuredness and confidence, thereby increasing the chances of your physical performance aligning with your mental projection.

Negative emotions are part of the human experience and can surface when we don't perform as expected or make a mistake. However, these feelings can be harnessed and redirected for positive outcomes.

Evaluating Performance

Rather than letting frustration or disappointment pull you down, use these emotions as an opportunity for introspection and performance analysis. Reflect on what went wrong and what you could have done differently, and formulate strategies to avoid making the same mistakes in the future. This productive use of negative emotions can foster personal growth and lead to improved performance on the course.

Avoiding Needless Self-Criticism: Building a Positive Self-Image

Self-criticism is a double-edged sword. Constructive self-critique can lead to self-improvement; however, destructive self-criticism can erode self-esteem and hinder performance. Be gentle with yourself when you make mistakes. Remember that learning is a process and that errors are simply stepping stones on the path to mastery. Make sure that your self-critique is aimed at helping you grow and is not designed to belittle or discourage you.

Returning to the Big Picture

Each shot you make, each hole you complete, and each round you play are components of a much bigger journey. It's easy to get caught up in the details of each game, but maintaining perspective can help preserve your positive mindset. Always keep your long-term goals in view, remember that each round provides you with a unique opportunity for growth, and appreciate the learning that comes with every game.

Remember the Reason You're Playing

Why are you out there on the golf course? Is it for the thrill of competition? For the joy of self-improvement? For camaraderie? Or simply for the love of the game? Never lose sight of the reasons why you play golf. This understanding can serve as a powerful motivator, especially during times of challenge or frustration.

Enjoying the Game

Ultimately, golf is a game, and the essence of games lies in the joy they bring. Savor every moment on the golf course: the triumphs, the challenges, and even the setbacks. Each experience is part of the rich tapestry of your golf journey. It's this appreciation and enjoyment of the game that will keep you returning to the tee with a positive mindset, ready to tackle the challenges anew.

By incorporating these strategies into your golfing mindset, the power of positive thinking will be more than just a concept. It will become a practical tool that can significantly boost your performance, enhance your enjoyment of the game, and turn every round of golf into a fulfilling experience.

Stories to Inspire: Tales of Triumph—Ally McDonald's Conquest Over Negativity

Picture this: You're in the middle of an intense golf game, your concentration unyielding, your grip firm. Suddenly, a small whisper of negativity creeps into your mind, disrupting your focus and shaking your confidence. Such moments of self-doubt aren't alien to even the best athletes, and while they can be disruptive, they can also be harnessed to turn the tide in your favor. The story of Ally McDonald, a celebrated golfer, beautifully illustrates this transformative journey.

Every golfer, irrespective of their skill level, grapples with negative thoughts. Ally, too, wasn't spared from these mental interferences. But what sets her apart is her remarkable ability to channel these thoughts into a win. At the 2020 LPGA Drive On Championship, McDonald faced one of her most formidable tests, yet she emerged victorious through the power of positive thinking. Ally was leading the tournament, but trouble brewed at the 17th hole where she made a bogey. For most players, this might have been the point of collapse, where negativity swarms in, doubts become monsters, and thoughts spiral into chaos. However, Ally's story took a different turn.

"I'm not going to lie, it shook me up pretty bad," Ally later confessed. She could have capitulated under the weight of the moment, but she didn't. Instead, she steadied her heart rate, pulled herself together, and reminded herself of a simple, yet powerful message: "Calm down and do what I've been doing every single round."

In that crucial moment, Ally acknowledged her negative thoughts, but didn't let them rule her. She allowed herself to feel the sting of her setback, but didn't allow it to destroy her game. Instead, she utilized it as fuel to regain her focus, and ultimately clinched the championship by a single stroke. But how did Ally manage to do this? How did she interrupt the negativity and refocus her mind on the game? It all boils down to a simple strategy, which we'll call the ABCD of positivity:

A - Awareness: Ally recognized the onset of negative thoughts. B - Breathe: She took a deep, calming breath. C - Calm: She stayed mentally and physically calm. D - Direct: She redirected her focus to the next shot.

By applying this strategy, Ally exemplified the fact that negative thoughts don't always spell disaster. It's about how you respond to them that truly counts. She transformed what could have been a downfall into a story of victory, a lesson in resilience that we can all take to heart.

Whether you're a teen learning the ropes of life, a parent guiding your child, or an athlete fighting for your dreams, remember Ally's story. It's proof that we have the power to turn negative thoughts into a win and that with a calm mind, a resilient spirit, and unwavering focus, we can achieve our goals, no matter the obstacles in our path.

Teeing Up: Actionable Steps to Improve Mental Toughness

For the Coach

1. Debunk the Positivity Myth: Explain that positivity is not just about focusing on the good and ignoring the bad. Stress the importance of understanding and accepting negative emotions as part of the process.

2. Promote Neutral Thinking: Encourage athletes to reframe negative thoughts into positive ones. Instead of shifting away from negative thoughts, teach them how to see these thoughts in a different light.

3. Highlight the Benefits of Positivity: Explain how a positive mindset can ease anxiety, influence the overall mindset, and impact performance on the golf course.

4. Teach Positive Visualization Techniques: Guide your players on how to visualize success and set their intentions before the game. Explain how these techniques can build confidence and improve focus.

5. Inspire with Success Stories: Share stories like Ally McDonald's, who channeled her negative thoughts into a win, to demonstrate the power of positivity in action.

For the Athlete

1. Understand the Positivity Myth: Know that positive thinking is not about ignoring the negatives but rather is about reframing them into something constructive.

2. Practice Neutral Thinking: Learn to put a positive spin on negative thoughts rather than ignoring them. This shift in perspective can significantly impact your performance.

3. Recognize the Power of Positivity: Understand how a positive mindset can shape your performance on the golf course, ease anxiety, and even influence those around you.

4. Visualize Success: Use visualization techniques to imagine your success on the golf course. Focus on what you want to achieve, not on what you fear might happen.

5. Channel Negative Emotion Productively: Instead of dwelling on negative emotions, use them to analyze and evaluate your performance. Remember the bigger picture, your larger goals, and why you're playing the game. Always keep in mind that golf is meant to be enjoyed.

Conclusion

Practicing positivity provides a nuanced perspective on the role of positivity in golf. Rather than subscribing to the misconception that positivity equates to overlooking the negatives, this chapter underscores the importance of adopting "neutral thinking," a more objective approach to the game that balances acknowledging difficulties and focusing on what's within your control. Emphasizing positivity's role in shaping our mindset, easing anxiety, and improving focus, it suggests that golf, ultimately, is a mental game requiring a positive attitude not only for a superior performance but also for a more enjoyable experience. Tips for fostering this mindset include setting intentions, visualizing success, using negative emotion productively, and maintaining sight of the bigger picture. As demonstrated by the inspiring story of Ally McDonald, embracing positivity in the face of challenges can indeed pave the way to success. Through this understanding, golfers are better equipped to enjoy the game, reinforce self-belief, and nurture resilience in the face of golf's inherent challenges.

Words of Wisdom to Players

"*Concentration comes out of a combination of confidence and hunger.*"—Arnold Palmer (USA Today Sports, 2016)

"*Success in golf depends less on the strength of body and more on the strength of mind and character.*"—Arnold Palmer (19tHole, 2021)

"*Golf is a puzzle without an answer. I've played the game for 40 years, and I still haven't the slightest idea of how to play.*"—Gary Player (CoolNSmart, n.d.)

"*I never learned anything from a match that I won.*"—Bobby Jones (Goodreads, n.d.)

"*The most rewarding things you do in life are often the ones that look like they cannot be done.*"—Arnold Palmer (Abed, 2018)

"*I get to play golf for a living. What more can you ask for, getting paid for doing what you love.*"—Tiger Woods (BrainyQuotes, n.d.-h)

"*It's not just the game I love, it's the life it leads you to. A life spent in pursuit of excellence, not perfection.*"—Ben Hogan (QuoteFancy, 2023)

"Golf is a difficult game, but it's a little easier when you trust your instincts. It's too hard a game to try to play like someone else."—Nancy Lopez (QuoteFancy, n.d.-d)

"No one will ever have golf under his thumb. No round ever will be so good it could not have been better. Perhaps this is why golf is the greatest of games."—Bobby Jones (Oscarson, n.d.)

"Golf is a game of precision, not strength. Power is a part of the game, certainly, but precision is what counts most."—Jack Nicklaus (Brett Avery Photos, 2010)

"To me, the game of golf is not just a physical exercise; it's a mental exercise. It's about controlling my thoughts, my nerves, my emotions, and most of all, my ego."—Arnold Palmer (Stabler, 2020)

"Golf is a game in which you yell 'fore', shoot six, and write down five."—Paul Harvey (BrainyQuotes, n.d.-d)

"Golf is not just an exercise; it's an adventure, a romance... a Shakespeare play in which disaster and comedy are intertwined."—Harold Segall (FunSaaz, n.d.)

"The object of golf is not just to win. It is to play like a gentleman and win."—Phil Mickelson (BrainyQuotes, n.d.-e)

"A bad attitude is worse than a bad swing."—Payne Stewart (QuoteFancy, n.d.-e)

"You don't know what pressure is until you play for five bucks with only two bucks in your pocket."—Lee Trevino (BrainyQuotes, n.d.-c)

"Golf is a spiritual game. It's like Zen. You have to let your mind take over."—Amy Alcott (BrainyQuotes, n.d.-a)

"Don't force your kids into sports. I never was. To this day, my dad has never asked me to go play golf. I ask him. It's the child's desire to play that matters, not the parent's desire to have the child play."—Tiger Woods (BrainyQuotes, n.d.-g)

"The game of golf doesn't come rushing back to you. Last week I made a couple of fundamental mistakes that I probably wouldn't have made in the heat of the battle back when I was in my heyday, and those things have got to come back."—Greg Norman (WhatShouldIReadNext, n.d.)

"I never go on a golf course without thanking the Lord for the opportunity to walk around out there."—Byron Nelson (Britannica, 2023)

"Golf is a game that requires a huge amount of mental concentration."—Ian Poulter (MacKenzie, 2016)

"Golf is a game where white men can dress up as black pimps and get away with it."—Robin Williams (QuoteFancy, n.d.-f)

"Golf is a day spent in a round of strenuous idleness."—William Wordsworth (Golfcare, 2018)

"Golf is not a fair game, so why build a course fair?"—Pete Dye (PictureQuotes, n.d.)

"It takes hundreds of good golf shots to gain confidence, but only one bad one to lose it."—Jack Nicklaus (QuoteFancy, n.d.-c)

"I can always make birdie on the last hole to win. But if I have to make birdie to tie, I'll choke every time."—Lou Graham (Tom Callahan Photos, 2013)

"Golf is assuredly a mystifying game. It would seem that if a person has hit a golf ball correctly a thousand times, he should be able to duplicate the performance at will. But such is certainly not the case."—Bobby Jones (QuoteFancy, n.d.-a)

"Golf is a game, and games are meant to be enjoyed." - Raymond Floyd (BrainyQuotes, n.d.-f)

"Golf is a game you can never get too good at. You can improve, but you can never get to where you master the game." - Gay Brewer (QuotesFancy, n.d.-b)

Final Note to Coaches

Coaches, the essence of your job goes beyond simple guidance. You hold the power to shape mindsets, transform perceptions, and set the tone for how your players approach not just the game but life as a whole. Your role is instrumental in molding individuals who are resilient, determined, and adept at navigating life's highs and lows.

One of the most powerful lessons you can teach your team is the art of being present. The game, regardless of the sport, mirrors life's uncertainties, challenges, and opportunities. Every move, every decision, every victory, and every defeat carries weight. However, it's crucial to realize that the strength of a player lies not in dwelling on a missed shot or in anticipating the next one, but in dealing with the play right in front of them.

Encourage your players to develop a mindset of focus, one that is grounded in the present moment. A moment missed is a moment lost. Stress upon them the significance of each play, each moment, each decision. Help them understand the sheer power of "now," for in "now" lies the possibility of change, of transformation, of victory.

Yet, the teaching of such a philosophy is incomplete without its implementation in your personal life. As a coach, it's imperative that you lead by example. Show your players the power of embracing the present moment, of handling the play right in front of you. Display how a past setback doesn't determine the outcome of the present play and how an uncertain future doesn't detract from the importance of the current moment.

Live in the present. Play in the present. Guide in the present. When you do so, you don't just shape exceptional players, you mold individuals who understand the significance of now, who are equipped to handle life's challenges head-on, and who embrace each moment with determination and focus. In the end, this is more than a game. It's about preparing your players for the grand match of life.

References

19tHole. @19tHole_uk. (2021, December 1). *Success in golf depends less on the strength of body and more on the strength of mind and character! Arnold* [Tweet]. Twitter. https://twitter.com/19thole_uk/status/1465984117548490753

Abed, W.H. (2018, August 27). *The most rewarding things you do in life are often the ones that look like they cannot be done - Arnold Palmer*. LinkedIn. https://www.linkedin.com/pulse/most-rewarding-things-you-do-life-often-ones-look-abed-ltc-fic#:~:text=Arnold%20Palmer

BrainyQuotes. (n.d.-a). *Amy Alcott quotes*. BrainyQuote. https://www.brainyquote.com/quotes/amy_alcott_215944

BrainyQuotes. (n.d.-b). *Bobby Jones quotes*. BrainyQuote. https://www.brainyquote.com/quotes/bobby_jones_391177

BrainyQuotes. (n.d.-c). *Lee Trevino quotes*. BrainyQuote. https://www.brainyquote.com/quotes/lee_trevino_389561

BrainyQuotes. (n.d.-d). *Paul Harvey quotes*. BrainyQuote. https://www.brainyquote.com/quotes/paul_harvey_105400

BrainyQuotes. (n.d.-e). *Phil Mickelson quotes*. BrainyQuote. https://www.brainyquote.com/quotes/phil_mickelson_211142

BrainyQuotes. (n.d.-f). *Raymond Floyd quotes*. BrainyQuote. https://www.brainyquote.com/quotes/raymond_floyd_527132

BrainyQuotes. (n.d.-g). *Tiger Woods quotes-1*. BrainyQuote. https://www.brainyquote.com/quotes/tiger_woods_161480

BrainyQuotes. (n.d.-h). *Tiger Woods quotes-2*. BrainyQuote. https://www.brainyquote.com/quotes/tiger_woods_368910

Brett Avery Photos. (2010, June 2). *Jack Nicklaus: In his own words*. Golf Digest. https://www.golfdigest.com/story/jack-nicklaus-quotes

Britannica. (2023, May 17). *Byron Nelson*. Britannica. https://www.britannica.com/biography/Byron-Nelson

CoolNSmart. (n.d.). *Gary Player quote*. CoolNSmart. https://www.coolnsmart.com/quote-golf-is-a-puzzle-without-117298/

FunSaaz. (n.d.). *Best quotes by Harold Segall*. FunSaaz. https://funsaaz.com/authors/harold-segall/

Golf Care. (2018, October 16). *20 famous golf quotes to impress on the course*. The Golf Care Blog. https://www.golfcare.co.uk/blog/2018/10/famous-golf-quotes/#:~:text=

Goodreads. (n.d.). *Bobby Jones quote*. Goodreads https://www.goodreads.com/quotes/7979310-i-never-learned-anything-from-a-match-that-i-won

Heime, J. (2015, April 4). *Emotions run the show in golf*. Golfwrx. https://www.golfwrx.com/289363/emotions-run-the-show-in-golf/

MacKenzie, D. (2016, September 15). *7 ways to improve your golf focus*. The Golf State of Mind Blog. https://golfstateofmind.com/improve-focus-for-golf/

Oscarson, P. (2013, September 5). *10 quotes to help you in golf (and life)*. Bleacher Report. https://bleacherreport.com/articles/1763026-10-quotes-to-help-you-in-golf-and-life

PictureQuotes. (n.d.). *Pete Dye quote.* PictureQuotes. http://www.picturequotes.com/golf-is-not-a-fair-game-so-why-build-a-course-fair-quote-189698

QuoteFancy. (2023). *Top 50 Ben Hogan quotes.* QuoteFancy. https://quotefancy.com/ben-hogan-quotes

QuoteFancy. (n.d.-a). *Bobby Jones quote.* QuoteFancy. https://quotefancy.com/quote/1260651/Bobby-Jones-Golf-is-assuredly-a-mystifying-game-It-would-seem-that-if-a-person-has-hit-a

QuotesFancy. (n.d.-b). *Gay Brewer quote.* QuoteFancy. https://quotefancy.com/quote/1609489/Gay-Brewer-Golf-is-a-game-you-can-never-get-too-good-at-You-can-improve-but-you-can-never

QuoteFancy. (n.d.-c). *Jack Nicklaus quote.* QuoteFancy. https://quotefancy.com/quote/1344287/Jack-Nicklaus-It-takes-hundreds-of-good-golf-shots-to-gain-confidence-but-only-one-bad

QuoteFancy. (n.d.-d). *Nancy Lopez quote.* QuoteFancy. https://quotefancy.com/quote/1301728/Nancy-Lopez-Golf-is-a-difficult-game-but-it-s-a-little-easier-if-you-trust-your-instincts

QuoteFancy. (n.d.-e). *Payne Stewart quote.* QuoteFancy. https://quotefancy.com/quote/1429814/Payne-Stewart-A-bad-attitude-is-worse-than-a-bad-swing

QuotesFancy. (n.d.-f). *Robin Williams quote.* Quotefancy.com. https://quotefancy.com/quote/902227/Robin-Williams-Golf-is-a-game-where-white-men-can-dress-up-as-black-pimps-and-get-away

Stabler, J. (2020, May 20). *Emotional stability in golf: Understanding your emotions.* GolfPsych. https://www.golfpsych.com/emotional-stability-understanding-emotions/

Tom Callahan Photos. (2013, January 6). *That 70's show.* Golf Digest. https://www.golfdigest.com/story/tom-callahan-greatest-generation

USA Today Sports. (2016, September 26). *The best Arnold Palmer quotes*. USA Today. https://www.usatoday.com/story/sports/golf/2016/09/25/best-arnold-palmer-quotes/91101166/

WhatShouldIReadNext. (n.d.). *Greg Norman quote.* WhatShouldIReadNext? https://whatshouldireadnext.com/quotes/greg-norman-the-game-of-golf-doesn-t

Made in the USA
Las Vegas, NV
02 September 2023